KNOWING CHRISTIANITY

THE LIFE AND TEACHING OF JESUS

KNOWING CHRISTIANITY

A series edited by Dr. William Neil to provide for thinking laymen a solid but non-technical presentation of what the Christian religion is and what it has to say in this atomic age.

The first titles are:

THE CHRISTIAN FAITH

THE OLD TESTAMENT

THE LIFE AND TEACHING OF JESUS

KNOWING CHRISTIANITY

The Life and Teaching
of
Jesus

by

WILLIAM NEIL
D.D.
Warden of Hugh Stewart Hall,
University of Nottingham

J. B. LIPPINCOTT COMPANY
Philadelphia and New York

EDITOR'S PREFACE

To judge by the unending flow of religious literature from the various publishing houses there is an increasingly large demand on the part of ordinary intelligent people to know more about what Christianity has to say. This series is designed to help to meet this need and to cater for just this kind of people.

It assumes that there is a growing body of readers, both inside and outside the Church, who are prepared to give 'serious attention to the nature and claims of the Christian faith, and who expect to be given by theologians authoritative and up-to-date answers to the kind of questions thinking people want to ask.

More and more it becomes clear that we are unlikely to get any answers that will satisfy the deepest needs of the human spirit from any other quarter. Present-day science and philosophy give us little help on the ultimate questions of human destiny. Social, political and educational panaceas leave most of us unpersuaded. If we are not to end our quest for the truth about ourselves and the world we live in, in cynicism and disillusionment, where else can we turn but to religion?

Too often in the past two thousand years the worst advertisement for Christianity has been its supporters and advocates. Yet alone of all the great world religions it has shown that a faith which was oriental in origin could be transplanted into the western world and from there strike root again in the east. The present identification of Christianity in the minds of Asians and Africans with European culture and western capitalism or imperialism is a passing phase. To say that no other religion has the same potentialities as a world-wide faith for everyman is neither to denigrate the God-given truth in Buddhism, Islam and the rest, nor to say that at this stage

5

Christianity as generally practised and understood in the west presents much more than a caricature of its purpose.

Perhaps the best corrective to hasty judgment is to measure these two thousand years against the untold millions of years of man's development. Organized Christianity is still in its infancy, as is the mind of man as he seeks to grapple with truths that could only come to him by revelation. The half has not yet been told and the full implications for human thought and action of the coming of God in Christ have as yet been only dimly grasped by most of us.

It is as a contribution to a deeper understanding of the mystery that surrounds us that this series is offered. The early volumes deal, as is only right, with fundamental issues—the historical impact of Christianity upon mankind based upon its Jewish origins and establishing itself in the wider world; the essence of the Christian faith and the character of Christian behaviour. Later volumes in the series will deal with various aspects of Christian thought and practice in relation to human life in all its variety and with its perennial problems.

The intention is to build up over the years a library which under the general title of 'Knowing Christianity' will provide for thinking laymen a solid but non-technical presentation of what the Christian religion is and what it has to say in this atomic age.

The writers invited to contribute to this series are not only experts in their own fields but are all men who are deeply concerned that the gulf should be bridged between the specialized studies of the theologian and the untheologically minded average reader who nevertheless wants to know what theology has to say. I am sure that I speak in the name of all my colleagues in this venture when I express the hope that this series will do much to bridge the gap.

WILLIAM NEIL

The University,
Nottingham

AUTHOR'S PREFACE

WHEN I was an undergraduate the questions about Christianity that exercised my contemporaries and myself—at least those of us who were interested in talking about religion—appear to me now to have been peripheral. We discussed the gospel miracles, the Virgin Birth and so on, against a background of religious conviction and an established pattern of Church life which were then the stock in trade of 'well brought up' young men and women. My impression is that young people today who think about these matters put far more radical question marks against much more fundamental issues. They do not ask: Could Jesus walk on the Sea of Galilee? but rather: Has the idea of God any meaning at all? Yet sooner or later any questions about God, ourselves and the world we live in lead us to ask questions about Christ.

I can only express here briefly the conviction which I hope emerges from these pages that, whatever differences of opinion there may be about this or that aspect of the life and teaching of Jesus, Christ and Christ alone holds the key to the total meaning of life. More than that, I believe that any attempt to explain the mystery that surrounds the Carpenter of Nazareth which does not find the solution in terms of the Second Person of the Trinity does less than justice to the evidence of the New Testament, to the history of Christendom and to human experience.

Anyone who is rash enough to write a life of Jesus is only too well aware that he has undertaken an impossible task and is only too conscious of the vast variety of problems that he has left unanswered. Nevertheless in a series called *Knowing Christianity* this is one vital component which cannot be omitted. Perhaps too in the prevailing climate of opinion it may serve some purpose if a book on this subject is written

7

from a point of view which will appear to many to be too conservative. To some on the other hand it may appear to be not conservative enough.

I have tried to make plain in these chapters my feeling that it is basically no more difficult in the twentieth century than in any other for us to get from the New Testament a sufficiently clear picture of the life and teaching of Jesus. We shall certainly not arrive at such a picture in this or in any century by removing from the gospel record everything that for one reason or another appears to be out of harmony with contemporary trends of thought, though these must be taken into account. Nor on the other hand shall we arrive at it by blandly disregarding the results of sound and scholarly biblical criticism, though personal opinions and personal bias are bound to influence our conclusions. As far as the actual writing of a life of Jesus is concerned it is certain that at any stage in New Testament theological studies it will be at many points something of an interim report and I can think of no other subject which so completely demonstrates to an author his total inadequacy to do it justice.

I am grateful to the Editor of the *Expository Times* for permission to reprint the chapter on 'The Jesus of History' which has already appeared in that journal.

WILLIAM NEIL

The University,
Nottingham.
August, 1964.

CONTENTS

Chapter One

THE JESUS OF HISTORY

HERE are three quotations. The first is this: "The Jesus of Nazareth who came forward publicly as the Messiah, who preached the ethic of the Kingdom of God, who founded the Kingdom of Heaven upon earth, and died to give His work its final consecration never had any existence . . . He comes to us as one unknown, without a name, as of old by the lakeside He came to those men who knew Him not."

This is the second: "It seems then that the form of the earthly no less than the heavenly Christ is for the most part hidden from us. For all the inestimable value of the gospels they yield us little more than a whisper of His voice: we trace in them but the outskirts of His ways."

And the third: "I do indeed think that we can now know nothing concerning the life and personality of Jesus, since early Christian sources show no interest in either, are moreover fragmentary and often legendary, and other sources about Jesus do not exist."

These three quotations are not as some might think from the works of eighteenth-century rationalists or twentieth-century sceptics but from three devout Christian scholars, two of whom are still alive and of international reputation, Albert Schweitzer and Rudolf Bultmann, and the third, R. H. Lightfoot, until his death a few years ago, was among his other offices, examining chaplain to the Archbishop of Canterbury which is surely the hallmark of theological respectability.

It is thus not the view of some literary dilettantes, scientific humanists, or religious crackpots, but of three Christian scholars of undoubted piety and integrity that the Jesus of history is a will-o'-the-wisp, that there is little or nothing about the conventional and traditional portrait of Jesus that is justified by the evidence inside or outside the Bible, and that any life of Jesus in the ordinary sense simply cannot be written.

The Christ-Myth

Fifty years ago was the heyday of the Christ-myth. The exponents of this theory maintained that Jesus never really existed—that the gospels were pure fiction and that the Church was founded on an imaginary character with no more reality than any of the gods on Olympus. They argued that the Virgin Birth was paralleled in the legends of Buddha, Krishna and Mithras, that a dying and rising god was an article of belief among the worshippers of Adonis and Osiris, that the healing acts of Jesus were no more historical than those of Aesculapius, and that His teaching can be shown to be little different in many respects from other Jewish and Gentile ethical systems.

On these and similar grounds it was not altogether fantastic or irrational to claim that in the cult of Jesus we have simply another example of the human desire to escape from the harsh realities of life as it is, to a dream world which solves all problems. But the Christ-myth theory foundered on the rocks of hard facts. No serious historian today—Christian or non-Christian—would subscribe to the theory that Jesus never existed. The evidence is conclusive on any reasonable view that a man called Jesus lived in Palestine two thousand years ago, suffered under Pontius Pilate, was crucified, dead and buried. This much at least of the Apostles' Creed is not a matter for dispute.

There is obviously no reference in Roman official histories contemporary with Jesus to His activity or even to His existence. Religious cranks—for this was how the Romans regarded all Jewish and Christian teachers and preachers—only became news when the movements they inspired interfered with the business of government or with law and order.

This is precisely what happened in the case of Christianity. Pliny, Roman governor of Bithynia, who had trouble with

Christians in his province, wrote a letter to the Emperor Trajan about A.D. 110 in which he spoke of them "singing hymns to Christ as to a god". Tacitus in his Annals, writing about the same time of the persecution of Christians under Nero, says that "the originator of that name, Christ, was put to death in the reign of Tiberius by the procurator Pontius Pilate". Josephus, the Jewish historian of the first century spoke of "James, the brother of Jesus who was called Christ" and the Talmud refers to Jesus as a rabbi who gathered disciples round Him, was condemned for sorcery and for leading Israel astray and who was hanged on the eve of Passover.

Modern orthodox Jews, whatever they think of Christian doctrine, have never disputed the fact that Jesus lived and died at the time and in the setting that the gospels describe. The Christ-myth theory therefore cannot hold water. But to come back to our three theologians, are they right in saying that apart from the barest details the life of Jesus is a closed book?

Let us not be dazzled by Schweitzer's brilliance as a musician and his greatness as a medical missionary into accepting uncritically all that he has to say about the New Testament. When Schweitzer insists that the Jesus of history has no existence, as he does in his famous book *The Quest of the Historical Jesus*[1], he is protesting against the nineteenth and early twentieth century tendency to equate Jesus with a European gentleman of high moral principles, and against the whole school of muscular Christianity, Jesus the boy's hero, the great Elder Brother, and such like trivial interpretations of a figure whom Schweitzer recognized as enigmatic, dynamic, trenchant and complex, who could by no manner of means be fitted into the pedestrian western mould that was then the fashion.

What Schweitzer wanted to substitute, however, was a deluded fanatic who expected the end of the world, went to his death assuming that that would bring it about, and who said nothing that was of any significance for the kind of world in which ordinary men have to live. Schweitzer has done us

[1]pp. 396, 401.

a great service by calling attention to the strange and awkward and unfamiliar elements in the gospel which the conventional pictures of Jesus ignored, but his own picture is now generally recognized to be even more untrue and lop-sided and no scholar today subscribes to it.

To come to our second quotation. When R. H. Lightfoot claimed that all we can get from the gospels is the whisper of Jesus' voice[1] he was writing at a time, thirty years ago, when the latest fashion in German New Testament studies—Form-Criticism—was becoming generally known in this country. Among other things the form-critics stressed the fact that what we have in the gospels is preaching material and not history. The stories which we had always taken to be genuine reminiscences of what Jesus did were, they claimed, really a collection of carefully polished pearls strung together in no particular order, artificially cultured to meet the need of the early missionaries for illustrations and allusions in their sermons.

Undoubtedly Jesus had said and done things that were remembered, but, said the Form-Critics, the Church had had such a big hand in shaping the sayings and stories we find in the gospels that we cannot really talk in any sense of a Jesus of history, or hope to form a picture of what Jesus said and did that corresponds with the facts. All we can get is a picture of what the early Church believed about Jesus.

Here again, as in the case of Schweitzer, was something that needed to be said. The gospels are not potted biographies and the people who wrote them were not interested in the kind of tittle-tattle, childhood reminiscences, psychological development and so on that a modern biographer would naturally want to include. Jesus Himself wrote nothing down and by the time the gospels came to be written, the evangelists had to rely on what they heard from the people who had known Jesus and what they had been taught themselves as missionaries. None of this was history as we know it. Nothing like a

[1]*History and Interpretation in the Gospels*, p. 225.

14

full record of all that Jesus said and did was available to the gospel writers and everything that *was* available was coloured by the faith of men who believed that in the words and deeds of Jesus they had been brought face to face with God.

An Overstated Case

The Form-Critics—and Professor Lightfoot, their chief representative in this country—were right in reminding us that in the gospels we can never say with complete certainty: this is precisely what Jesus said or this is precisely what Jesus did. There is always the possibility of misunderstanding, or of faulty memories, or of exaggeration or of embellishment. Above all they were right to remind us that the gospels never provide us with plain hard facts without at the same time saying something about the meaning of these facts. We all know that it is impossible for a modern secular historian to be completely impartial. He is bound to give his own interpretation of the events he is describing.

The biblical writers do not even try to be impartial. They record the things that happened, not for their own sake, but because in one way or another they saw in them the hand of God at work. Above all in the gospels, in the life of Jesus, everything that is written down has passed through the minds of men who were convinced that Jesus of Nazareth was a unique person who came on to the stage of history by the direct intervention of God; that in Him God was present among men in a totally new way, that a new age had begun, a new power had come into the world, and that all this was the climax of two thousand years of preparation for His coming; that the hopes and prayers and failures and successes of the people whose story is recorded in the Old Testament now fitted into place; that this was in effect a new act of creation as significant as the one by which God brought the universe into being.

Could men who thought in this way be expected to write a prosaic matter of fact record of what actually happened?

Could they help but see everything that Jesus had said and done through the eyes of their own faith and conviction, linking it up with the Old Testament story, finding eternal significance in the things that Jesus had done and said, and only recording things that seemed to them to have this kind of significance?

But it is one thing to say all that and quite another to say that the gospels are simply what the gospel writers thought about Jesus and not what Jesus actually did and said. If the gospel writers wrote from the point of view that they were not recording a collection of facts about a dead prophet, or a heroic martyr, or an inspired teacher, but telling the good news of how God had come into everyday life, how did they reach that conclusion if the things Jesus said and did and the impression He made on them had not made such a conclusion inescapable?

When we read the gospels we are not reading a haphazard collection of sayings and stories used by missionaries and jumbled together like groceries in a shopping basket, but a coherent developing story of the life and teaching of a man who had lived and died in such a manner as to convince His followers that here in some mysterious and inexplicable way was someone who seemed to bring heaven to earth and lift earth to heaven. In other words we are dealing with an account of a historical person who said and did things of such an extraordinary character that the reflection of them can still be seen through the faith and devotion of the men who were His disciples.

Now let us look for a moment at the third quotation from our trio of theologians who tell us that we can never know the Jesus who walked and talked by the Lake of Galilee.[1] Rudolf Bultmann, who has a vast following on the Continent but less in this country, is obsessed by the notion that the life of Jesus is set in so mythological a framework that its real meaning can only be found when we get rid of the whole first century background and reduce the gospel to its essential feature—God

[1] *Jesus*, p. 11.

16

confronting man and calling for a decision, and man respond-
ing to God out of his existential situation.

In this process the basis for any life of Jesus disappears into
mythology—including the Virgin Birth, the miracles, the
Resurrection, the Ascension, the promise of the Second
Coming. These ideas, says Bultmann, belong to the Jewish
and Hellenistic world in which the gospel grew up and they
have no meaning for us today. Once we have got rid of them
we are left with a fairly ordinary Jewish prophet whom yet
by faith we recognise as God's own Son.

Once again we are up against a good but overstated case.
There is a mythological element in the gospels. It is quite
true for example that we no longer live in a world where illness
is reckoned to be caused by demon-possession. We do not
think of a three-storied universe with heaven above the sky
and hell below the earth. Jesus and His disciples were first
century Jews and what they did and said has to be translated
into twentieth century language if we are to understand it.

But once again we have to guard against throwing the baby
out with the bath water. The faith of the Church as expressed
in the creeds is founded on history, not on mythology. The
Jewish and Hellenistic environment in which Jesus lived and
the Church grew up cannot be dismissed as meaningless. We
have to come to terms with it, try to understand it and then
translate it into our own idiom. And if we say that the miracles,
the Resurrection, and the rest are part of the mythological
framework of the gospel we are left with the position that we
stand up and recite a creed which we know to be little more
than an elaborate theological fairy-tale.

Bultmann coins a new word 'demythologizing' the gospel to
mean what older generations meant by radical scepticism.
Many of us may find it impossible to see how Bultmann and
his disciples can combine such a sceptical view of the historical
value of the gospels with a full-blooded acceptance of the
traditional Christian faith. This has always been a tight-rope
act which the Germans seem to be able to accomplish very

successfully but it is a journey which less adventurous Anglo-Saxons find hazardous in the extreme.

But surely one must go farther and say that the scepticism represented by the three theologians already mentioned is largely unjustified. While we recognize a measure of truth behind each of their viewpoints, there is not the slightest reason for saying that the Jesus of history is unknowable and that we cannot talk in any realistic way about His life and teaching. On the contrary we have ample material in the New Testament not only for arriving at a picture of Christ as seen through the eyes of faith as the Saviour of the world, but also for arriving at a picture of Jesus the carpenter of Nazareth whose deeds and words were of such a character that His followers had no alternative but to call Him Son of God.

Grounds for Confidence

Let us look at the evidence of the New Testament. The Crucifixion took place in A.D. 29 or 30. A few weeks after it, according to the Book of Acts, the first Christian missionaries went out into the streets of Jerusalem to proclaim their faith that Jesus the carpenter of Nazareth was the Messiah to whom the whole story of the Old Testament pointed; that this was proved by the things He had done and the things He had said and above all by the fact that God had raised Him from the dead.

With this gospel—not like some devoted followers of a dead prophet but as men inspired by a risen and living Lord—these missionaries spread from Jerusalem throughout the Levant into Asia Minor and Europe until they had established Christian communities in the capital of the Roman Empire and in most strategic centres of the civilized world within about fifty years.

The missionary Paul of Tarsus, whose letters we have in the New Testament, the earliest of them dating from about twenty years after the Crucifixion, tells us what he himself was told about Jesus when he was converted to Christianity about three years after Jesus' death. The oldest gospel, St.

18

Mark, the first attempt to give a full account of the life and work of Jesus, was written in or around A.D. 65. There is good reason to believe that much of it is based on information derived from Peter the Galilean fisherman. The rest of the gospel —the framework of the life of Jesus—is what St. Mark, in common with all other Christian missionaries, had been told when he first became a Christian. The whole gospel is really an expansion of the little sermon summaries which the Book of Acts gives us as having been the message of the apostles in Jerusalem when the mission started on the first Whitsunday.

The teaching of Jesus, which has been collected in Matthew and Luke, was first gathered together before St. Mark's gospel was written—perhaps about A.D. 50—and bears every mark of being the words of a single creative mind, whose sayings were constructed in such a way that they could be easily remembered and used for the instruction of new converts. That is to say that within about thirty to forty years of the Crucifixion we have written records of the life and teaching of Jesus and behind them a preaching tradition of the same words and deeds which takes us right back to Jerusalem a few weeks after Jesus' death.

When we remember that oriental memories—especially those of trained teachers—are incomparably more retentive than our own, when we remember that when the first gospel was written there were still plenty of people alive who were contemporary with Jesus and could have easily exposed it as a fraud if it had not been largely true, and above all when we contrast our gospels with the fantastic legendary excesses of the lives of Jesus that came to be written in the second century, we can have every confidence that whatever allowances are made for occasional misunderstanding or pious exaggeration or other embellishments, the picture of Jesus that the gospels paint for us is basically reliable and historically accurate.

To say that we can know no more than that Jesus was a prophet who was crucified under Pontius Pilate is therefore not only defeatist but unscientific. The creeds of the Church are not elaborate dogmatic structures resting on subjective piety, wish-fulfilment or the hope that is born of despair, but like the gospels themselves they are human and inadequate attempts to express the inexpressible, to encase in cold words the impact on the world of a person who defies definition, who transcends the ordinary limits of human understanding but who still emerges plainly from the pages of the New Testament as one whom we can know as man and worship as God.

If Jesus is anything like what the Church has acclaimed Him for two thousand years to be, and if the experience of millions of men and women of all races, classes, ages and periods within that time is not to be dismissed as sheer delusion, then the picture that we should find in the gospels is that of a man who says what no ordinary man has ever said, who does what no ordinary man has ever done, and who somehow while being obviously as normal a human being as any carpenter of Nazareth must be, is at the same time so different from any other carpenter or any other man who ever lived as to reach at times beyond the limit of rational understanding and cold logic, and to be grasped only by the intuitive perception of poet and painter.

This mingling of the prosaic and the transcendent is precisely what the gospels provide—a picture of a man who knows hunger and weariness, disappointment and pain, yet who at the same time shows by what He says and does that His true home lies in another dimension and that He is able to offer a new quality of life based on this twin-allegiance—to the world and to God—to all who are prepared to commit themselves to Him and become His followers.

Chapter Two

THE PREACHING OF THE GOSPEL

LET us look first of all in more detail at the material from which any life of Jesus must be constructed, the four gospels, for if we cannot satisfy ourselves that these New Testament writings are an honest attempt to record the words and deeds and general impact of a historical person we might as well admit that no life of Jesus can ever be written. If the most we can expect is to detect a dim shadowy figure behind the accumulated faith and piety of the early Church, an unknowable and not particularly remarkable Jewish prophet or teacher, it is difficult to think that this would have been enough to launch and sustain a movement that despite all the faults and failures of its supporters still claims the allegiance of millions of men and women of all races in a totally different modern world.

The Old Testament is the literary deposit of religiously minded men within a particular nation. It is the product of the realization over a period of two thousand years by the priests and prophets of Israel of how God makes Himself known to man and of how He can be known by man. This is expressed in a great variety of literary forms from the primitive camp fire story and minstrel ballad to the highly developed oracles of the prophets, the prayers of the psalmists and the insights of the wisdom scribes.

The New Testament is also a literary deposit, not of a nation but of a community which is essentially supra-national. It is the product not of two thousand years but of a hundred years, and it was written by men who were without exception not religious littérateurs but men who were moved by the conviction that a new age had dawned and whose aim was to spread this knowledge throughout the world. In their view the climax of history had begun. God who had spoken in times past through the prophets had now Himself appeared on earth in the person of Jesus Christ.

This was a fact, the implications of which were so shattering that the men who had grasped them had no alternative but to proclaim them. There is a note of urgency throughout the whole of the New Testament. The decisive hour has come. So the writers are first and foremost missionaries, men with a message. Thus while it is true up to a point to say that behind the Old Testament lay the Jewish Church, it is much more true to say that behind the New Testament lies the Christian Church and that without the Church there would be no New Testament.

It is not the documents that comprise it that are primary and fundamental but the fact of Jesus Christ which gave them birth. The New Testament is the title deeds of Christ, an account of certain historical events and the explanation of their meaning. It is the result of the impact of Christ upon a little group of men in Palestine who formed the nucleus of the Christian Church. It is their attempt to describe that impact and what it meant for them and for the world. The very nature of the message compelled them to spread it further.

The motive behind the writing of the whole of the New Testament is thus largely a practical one. So the gospels are not written from a biographical point of view as we know it today. We look in vain there for the kind of details about Jesus that any modern biographers would inevitably include, details of His looks, His dress, His education, His accent. Not only are matters like these not mentioned, but the whole course of His life for thirty years is glossed over, with the exception of one small snippet at the age of twelve.

The gospels were written in order that men might come to see that Jesus of Nazareth was the Son of God. Behind all the incidents and sayings which are recorded there is this evangelical purpose. So it is with the New Testament letters. These are no ordinary items of correspondence full of small talk and personalities, but missionary propaganda often at white heat, written by men whose aim is to make Christ as vital a force in the lives of others as He had become in their own. It is thus fundamental to realize that the New Testament as we have it today came into being through the preaching of the Word.

The Making of the New Testament

As in the case of the Old Testament, the order in which the books of the New Testament appear in our Bibles is not the order in which they were written. St. Paul's letters, for example, dating from approximately A.D. 50-60, were written before the gospels as we have them in their present finished state. Within the first century of the Christian era, however, the New Testament as as we know it was practically complete, though for the early Christians it was not regarded as part of the Bible.

For them the Bible was the Old Testament and for a long time there was nothing else. Jesus wrote no Scriptures. He had regarded the Old Testament as the divinely inspired writings that pointed to His own coming and now that He had gone from the earth the Old Testament became doubly sacred to the Church. They searched the Scriptures to find passages which foretold the coming of a Saviour and they interpreted them in the light of their own knowledge and experience of Christ. That knowledge and experience was also something that at first needed no committing to paper. It was preached as a living message to Jews and Gentiles wherever the Christian missionaries went.

So it came about that when St. Paul, around A.D. 50, started the practice of writing letters to churches he was unable to visit at the time, he was unconsciously laying the foundations of the New Testament. Little Christian communities were soon scattered all over the Mediterranean world, in Rome, Greece and Asia Minor as well as in Palestine and Syria. St. Paul, active as he was, could not hope to cover all the ground.

Many problems arose in these Christian communities which needed his advice and so he devised the expedient of sending them letters. In those days there was no regular postal service except for official mail. Private individuals had to send their letters by hand.

Thus, from wherever he happened to be, and sometimes it was in prison, the great apostle kept up a steady flow of correspondence to Churches he had founded or hoped to visit. Some of these letters have been lost. Some have been preserved and now find a place in the New Testament. They reached that status not by any formal decree on the part of the Church, in the first instance at any rate. Their first stage was that they were read during the services in the churches to which they were addressed as a more or less informal pastoral message after the normal Old Testament scripture reading and exposition.

Then they came to be passed round the various little Christian communities, and as their importance was more and more recognized their status rose accordingly. Before the end of the first century most of the other letters in the New Testament came to be written in the same way. Meantime the gospels were coming into existence. For reasons which we shall see later the need was felt to commit to writing what had previously been passed on by word of mouth.

The first gospel to appear was that of St. Mark, in or about A.D. 65, to be followed soon after by the gospels of St. Matthew and St. Luke. These were not, as it were, rival compositions produced in the same spot. Originally they came from three distinct Christian communities. But as in the case of the epistles they were circulated round the churches and gradually came to be universally known. So it was with the fourth gospel, St. John, probably later than the other three, but well before the end of the century.

By about A.D. 100 practically all of the New Testament as we know it was in existence. It had not been written with a view to being collected. Each separate item was produced in some Christian community to meet some special need. But once they were in circulation their value became increasingly apparent. Each little church had its own library and copies of St. Paul's letters and of the gospels came to be prized more and more as time went on. There were other competitors for inclusion among the sacred writings of the Church which appeared in the second century A.D. and there was much discussion before a final decision was reached, following the lead of Athanasius in A.D. 367 who defined the New Testament exactly as we have it now.

The Need for a Canon

The formation of the canon of the New Testament, i.e. its officially authorized contents, was, like that of the Old Testament, a democratic process though accomplished in a much shorter time. The official tests were that a book should have been in regular use in all the churches and that it should be of apostolic origin. As in the case of the Old Testament, however, the real criterion was on the whole a book's own intrinsic merit. Nothing of real value was excluded from the New Testament on the grounds that it did not come up to the required specification, and much that was rejected was obviously rightly so dealt with.

The best proof of the inspired judgment of the early Church on this question is to compare our four canonical gospels with some of the apocryphal gospels which appeared in the second century and later. Such, for example, was the gospel of Peter, which was written from the viewpoint that the Christ could not suffer pain. He is therefore miraculously taken up to heaven from the Cross. Perhaps from the same gospel comes an account of the birth of Jesus, where He appears as a bright light which gradually takes the form of a child. The child has no weight and His eyes dazzle all who look at Him.

Other apocryphal gospels provide similarly fantastic information about Jesus' birth and boyhood. He makes clay sparrows which come to life when He claps His hands; a boy who knocks into Him falls dead; a young man has been changed by witchcraft into a mule but when Mary puts Jesus on the mule's back the youth becomes human again. Stories like these make us realize afresh the restraint and honesty with which our four gospels have been compiled.

It was of course partly because of the growth of spurious books of this kind that the need was felt to have an authoritative list of the official scriptures of the Christian Church. Another reason was the necessity to have a clearly defined doctrinal textbook from which to refute the various heresies which from the second century onwards threatened to distort beyond recognition the original faith of the apostles.

A True Text

Almost nineteen centuries have passed since the New Testament was first put into writing. The books were generally dictated to scribes, which might give rise to errors through incorrect hearing. Then for centuries, until the invention of printing, they were copied from one manuscript to another, with inevitable copyist's errors. How then have we any guarantee that what we read in the New Testament today corresponds at all with what was originally dictated? The work of biblical textual scholars who have subjected the oldest manuscripts of the New Testament to close scrutiny over the past century has ensured that no ancient documents have been so meticulously sifted, checked and cross-checked. There are altogether now available for scholarly investigation about four thousand manuscripts of the New Testament or of parts of it coming from different centres of Christianity in the early centuries of its history.

In addition there are copies of various translations from the original Greek into local languages and dialects, some of them older than the Greek manuscripts themselves. They indicate that the text of the oldest complete manuscripts, dating from the fourth century, is essentially the same as what these versions were translated from two centuries earlier. A third

26

method of corroboration is through the quotations from the books of the New Testament in commentaries and similar works by early Christian writers from the second century onwards. Substantially these quotations are identical with our New Testament today.

As a result of this threefold system of cross-checking—to say nothing of the additional evidence more recently supplied by discoveries of very early papyrus fragments of the New Testament writings going back to about A.D. 140—we can say that we have to all intents and purposes the same New Testament as was in use in the early Church not much more than a century after the death of Christ. It has been reckoned that after the most thorough-going textual criticism, analysis of sources and comparison of versions, only about one word in sixty in the New Testament is doubtful, and of these doubtful readings only again one out of sixty makes any difference to the sense.

Matthew, Mark, Luke and John, the four canonical gospels, are thus our textbooks for knowing the life and teaching of Jesus. The word Gospel, which can mean these four New Testament books or any one of them, is of Anglo-Saxon origin and means the good story or the God story. It is a translation of the Greek word *euangelion* (Latin—*evangelium*) which means Good News. It is worth emphasizing this meaning of the word Gospel because it helps us to understand its earliest characteristic, which was that it was proclaimed. The first stage of the gospels as we know them is that they came into being through the preaching of the Good News.

St. Mark's gospel, which as we shall see was the earliest of the four, was written somewhere about A.D. 65. Jesus was crucified about A.D. 30. What happened in the interval? Was there a vacuum of thirty years of which nothing is known until suddenly St. Mark's gospel makes its appearance? If so, why should it be necessary all at once for first one gospel then the others to appear? Let us then consider the answers to these questions under three main heads: What was the earliest form of the gospels? How did the present gospels emerge? Why did they emerge?

Oral Tradition

Christianity was from the beginning a missionary religion. It was never an esoteric philosophy of life. It was Good News about God and man that had to be proclaimed and therefore the origin of the gospels is to be sought in the preaching of the early Church. This preaching mission was begun by the apostles in Jerusalem on the first Whitsunday as recorded in Acts 2. What did they say? We find summaries of St. Peter's sermons about this time reproduced by St. Luke in the book of Acts which he wrote as a sequel to his gospel (Acts 2. 14–39; 3. 13–26; 4. 10–12; 5. 30–32; 10. 36–43). There is also a summary of a sermon by St. Paul in Acts 13. 17–41 and in the apostles's own letters there are certain passages which seem to indicate that he is quoting the generally accepted terms of the new Christian message (e.g. 1 Cor. 15. 1–7; Rom. 1. 1–4; 10. 8–9).

Out of these various passages it appears that the skeleton form of the most primitive preaching was on these lines:

(a) The Old Testament scriptures are now fulfilled. The promises made there have come true.

(b) The Messiah, the new David, has appeared.

(c) The Messiah is Jesus of Nazareth who went about doing good and performing mighty works by the power of God; who was crucified according to the purpose of God and was raised by God from the dead; who is exalted by God and given the name Lord; who will come again to judge all things.

(d) Therefore all who hear this message should repent and be baptized.

It is important to realize from this that the first Christian propaganda immediately after the Resurrection was not concerned with the recounting of personal mannerisms and

28

obiter dicta of Jesus—like Johnson interpreted by Boswell—
but the much more vital and startling claim that the long
promised Messianic Kingdom had arrived, the Messiah had
appeared, had died and risen again, and would shortly return
for the great Day of Judgment.

It is therefore a very strong conjecture that as all the early
preaching was directed towards the conversion of Jews, and
since the Bible for both Jews and Christians was the same Old
Testament, the earliest kind of literary product of the Christian
Church was a collection of passages drawn from the Old
Testament and designed to show that what had just happened
in Jerusalem to the person of Jesus of Nazareth was exactly
what the prophets had foretold would happen to the Messiah
when He came. Echoes of this probable original sub-stratum
of Christian literature can be seen in St. Matthew's gospel
where he repeatedly produces Old Testament quotations to
back up his narrative of the events in the life of Jesus.

It is sometimes argued by anti-Christian propagandists that
the true explanation of these Old Testament quotations in St.
Matthew and elsewhere is that the early Church simply
constructed a picture of what the Old Testament Messiah
would be like and then proceeded to invent details in Jesus'
life to fit them. That is surely psychologically incredible.
Unless the events of Jesus' life had suggested irresistibly a
comparison with some of the things that had been said of the
coming Messiah, it means that as soon as Jesus was dead the
process of concocting a pious fraud began and that the first
Christian missionaries went cheerfully to a martyr's death for
something they knew to be a lie. Furthermore, the kind of
Messiah that Jesus had turned out to be was in several important respects radically different from what the Old Testament writers had taught people to expect.

If we look at St. Mark's gospel, the earliest of the four, we
are at once struck by the disproportionate amount of space
devoted to the story of Christ's Trial and Death. The original
account must have been even longer still, since the last part of

the gospel dealing with the Resurrection has probably been lost. But even as it stands one-fifth of Mark deals with Passion Week and more than half the gospel follows on from Jesus' own pronouncement on the kind of death the future held for Him after St. Peter had acclaimed Him as the Messiah at Caesarea Philippi (8. 31).

The chief characteristic of St. Mark's gospel is its staccato style. One incident follows another not as if it were woven into a continuous narrative but as if the author had a number of unconnected anecdotes which he is stringing together. Now this does not apply to the Passion narrative. It is a coherent whole that gives the impression of having been a unity from the very beginning. And the Passion narrative is precisely the historical equivalent of the missionary preaching. It gives chapter and verse for the missionaries' claim that Jesus was the Messiah, that He had been crucified, had risen again and was exalted to the right hand of God.

It would seem then that side by side with proof texts from the Old Testament pointing to a coming Messiah went a historical narrative of Jesus' Passion purporting to show that the Death and Resurrection of the historical figure of Jesus of Nazareth did in fact fulfil these prophecies.

Another element in the early preaching is reflected in the words: "Jesus of Nazareth went about doing good and performing mighty acts by the power of God." The most natural thing that one would expect from the first missionaries would be that their sermons would be studded with illustrative incidents from the life of Jesus, showing how He healed the sick, befriended the sinner, made the blind see and the lame walk. These were all signs that the Kingdom of God had come. These evidences of divine power in Jesus corroborated the claim which the preachers made that this was indeed the Messiah. They were the prelude to the Passion.

So at this early stage we may assume that there was an outline of Jesus' ministry in a more or less fixed form current among the first missionaries, and that within this outline

30

there were various incidents in His life calculated to strengthen the conviction of the audience that the Good News was true. This seems to be indicated by the summaries in Acts 2. 22 and 10. 38.

Jesus came preaching that the Kingdom of God had come and teaching the kind of life that should be lived in it. It was natural that in the preaching of the early missionaries the teaching of Jesus should be passed on. It would be used for the instruction of children, it would be used in controversy with Jews and Gentiles, and above all it would be used by the new Christian communities themselves. Life for them was full of problems. How should they behave towards the Jews, towards the Roman authorities? Should they fast, should they eat with Gentiles—how far in short should the old practices of Judaism be carried over into Christianity?

For all such questions, as well as deeper questions of faith and sacraments Jesus had an answer. So these "words of the Lord" as St. Paul calls them, came to acquire in the early Church a status equal to that of the Old Testament. They were a final authority beyond which there was no higher (cf. Acts 20. 35; 1 Cor. 7. 10; 1 Cor. 11. 23 ff.).

Thus for the first twenty years of the Church's existence, i.e. A.D. 30–50, it is probable that the only written material in circulation was perhaps the collection of Old Testament proof texts, and that apart from that the gospels existed only in the form of oral tradition. The whole matter is up to a point conjectural. No one knows for certain whether small collections of the various types of stories and sayings may not have existed in written form in these early days, or whether the Passion narrative may not have been circulating in writing at this time too.

On the whole, however, it seems more likely that the first stage of the gospels was a pre-literary period when all that was known was so fresh and vivid that there was no need to write it down. The missionaries were doubtless carefully instructed in the traditional Jewish way by memorizing and by endless

31

repetition, and the safeguard exercised by the community against any missionary departing from the normal words of a saying or a narrative is in such circumstances similar to the protest of the small child if the favourite bed-time story is altered in any detail. The period of oral tradition in the case of the gospels was probably at the most twenty years. We can therefore safely assume that in that short time well-trained Jewish–Christian memories, especially when they were conscious of the revolutionary character of the gospel, reproduced with comparative accuracy what Jesus actually said and did.

Chapter Three

THE FOUR EVANGELISTS

Written Collections

TURNING now to the second question, How did the present gospels emerge?, it seems certain that at some time before the appearance of St. Mark's gospel in approximately A.D. 65, a start had been made to collect in written form selections of the various types of oral tradition in circulation. This may well have taken place between A.D. 50–65. It may indeed have been earlier. From the arrangement of St. Mark's gospel such a development is indicated. For example there is the series of incidents in which Jesus counters the opposition of the religious leaders in Mark 2. 1–3, 6 and 11. 27–12. 34, the so-called 'conflict stories'.

It looks as if these stories, illustrating as they do a growing hostility towards Jesus on the part of the religious authorities of the day, may have existed independently before St. Mark included them in his gospel. There is also what looks like an early collection of apocalyptic utterances in Mark 13, known as the 'Little Apocalypse'. In addition there may also have been some attempt to collect selections of the parables. When we remember that the primary function of the Church was to make converts, the usefulness from the evangelist's point of view of such collections for preaching purposes is self-evident.

Whatever doubt there may be about the existence of other written collections, there is almost unanimity among scholars about the appearance in this period of a collection of Jesus' sayings. Papias, an early bishop of the Church (*c.* A.D. 60–135), some of whose observations are preserved by Eusebius, a church historian of the fourth century, tell us that "Matthew compiled the oracles in the Hebrew dialect and each interpreted

33

them as he was able." The general view held now is that the Gospel according to St. Matthew was not written by one of the twelve apostles for reasons that we shall see. St. Matthew the apostle, however, may well have been, as Papias says, the editor of an early collection of the teaching of Jesus, assuming that this is what the word 'oracles' means.

When we come to look at our four gospels more closely we shall see that St. Matthew's gospel and St. Luke's gospel have in common a large number of sayings of Jesus. This shared material has such a large degree of verbal correspondence that it is universally agreed that they must have drawn this from a common source. This common source, known as Q (from the German word *quelle* = source) is obviously earlier than either of these two gospels and it may be that it is the collection of sayings which, according to Papias, St. Matthew first wrote down in Aramaic and which afterwards were translated into Greek.

Various copies would be put into circulation, one of which came into the hands of St. Luke, another into the hands of the author of the First Gospel. It is thought that Q was first produced at Antioch, perhaps as early as A.D. 50, but certainly before the gospel of St. Mark appeared in A.D. 65. No copies of it exist by themselves but from a study of its contents in Matthew and Luke it transpires that this is just the kind of document that would be useful for missionaries in instructing converts from among the Gentiles. Such a need would naturally arise at Antioch, the great nursery of the early Church in Syria, where the disciples were first called Christians (Acts 11. 26). Similar examples of collections of sayings of Jesus, some of them not found in the gospels, have been found in Egypt written on papyrus, indicating the way in which oral tradition has gradually become written tradition.

The Appearance of the Gospels

In the preface to St. Luke's gospel (1. 1) the author says: "Forasmuch as many have taken in hand to draw up a narrative concerning those matters which have been fulfilled

34

among us . . ." This seems to indicate that various attempts had been made to write a gospel along the lines which St. Luke himself follows. If that is so we have now no trace of them. The one certain fact is that the first man to write a gospel in our sense of the word was John Mark whose book now comes second in the New Testament.

Once more Bishop Papias has something to say on the subject. His comment is that: "Mark, the interpreter of Peter, wrote down accurately yet not in order all that he (Peter) told as said or done by Christ. For he (Mark) himself did not hear the Lord nor was a disciple of His, but of Peter, who used to give teachings to suit the immediate wants (of his hearers), but not as making a connected narrative."

The impression one gets from this is of the Apostle Peter, the rough Galilean fisherman, speaking mainly Aramaic, being accompanied on his preaching expeditions by a young secretary who was able to translate his message into Greek. Tradition brings them together to Rome where St. Peter like St. Paul was martyred in the great persecution of the Christians in A.D. 64. The Emperor Nero was responsible for this as for so many other crimes. The Christians were the most convenient scapegoats to cover up the cause of a fire that destroyed more than half of Rome, which many said had been started by the mad emperor himself.

Shortly after St. Peter's death there appeared this little book called 'The Gospel of Jesus Christ the Son of God' or as we now know it 'St. Mark's Gospel'. It was the first attempt to bring together all the floating tradition that existed concerning Jesus. Undoubtedly much of it was first-hand information from St. Peter, reminiscences gathered from his conversation, sermon illustrations, quoted sayings of Jesus, all prefaced to the current narrative of the Passion and put into the framework of the preaching of the Good News which by this time was common property. As we shall see, at least two of the remaining three gospels depend to a large extent on this gospel of John Mark.

35

Our third question was, Why did the gospels emerge at all? and once again St. Luke's preface suggests the clue. In it (1. 2) he speaks of "the original eye-witnesses and servants of the Gospel" who from the beginning had handed on the traditions concerning Jesus. These 'servants of the Gospel', the earliest missionaries, were of course the disciples, both those in the inner circle of the Twelve, and those who had been on the fringe.

These were the men who had been with Jesus, who had lived with Him, who had seen with their own eyes all that had happened and who because of that went out into all the world to preach the Gospel. Wherever they went and whatever they said they gave the impression of being first-hand authorities. They spread no carried tales but spoke from their own experience. So long as there were men alive who had taken part in these great events there was no need for written documents. Their testimony was the living word.

But with the passing of a generation the eye-witnesses began to die out and the Good News was spread at second hand. It was therefore a natural desire to want to commit to writing sayings of Jesus and incidents of His life while they were still fresh in the mind as they had been recounted by men who had been there.

There was also the rapid growth of the Church to be considered. Little communities were springing up in all the great cities of the Roman Empire as well as in Palestine, and not all the missionaries were as intrepid as St. Paul. It was therefore necessary to have something in writing for the use of those converts and catechumens who could not have the verbal instruction and inspiration of apostolic teachers and preachers. Oral tradition worked well enough in Palestine, in rural communities where people could neither read nor write, but in big cities where the pace of life was faster, memories were shorter, and outside distractions greater, it was safer to have things written down.

There was also the fact that the earliest Christians expected the almost immediate end of the world and the Second Advent of Christ. The Messiah had come as the prophets had foretold, but the Scriptures also promised a new heaven and a new earth. All the popular apocalyptic ideas of the time encouraged them to think that within the first generation after Jesus' Resurrection and Ascension, He would come again to judge the world and receive His own people to Himself. To men in this ferment of expectancy, or even to the more sober-minded who reckoned with it as a strong probability, the necessity for a written gospel did not arise. What had happened was but the prelude to the bigger things that were impending.

When St. Paul wrote his first letter to the Thessalonians about A.D. 50 he obviously shared this view. As time went on his outlook changed and this change was shared by the Church at large. It gradually became clear what Jesus had meant by His cryptic words about the future, and that not one generation but many more must pass before the final Judgment. With that realization came an enhanced appreciation of what had previously appeared to be rather trifling details in view of the expected cataclysm.

Life had to be lived in an increasingly complicated world. The problems of the present could not be shelved in the hope of a speedy solution from on high. So there was in consequence an increased desire to see what Jesus had actually said about His coming again, if He had indeed said anything at all about it and had not been totally misunderstood. And if they had to continue to live in a hostile world and do battle with the forces of evil, what had the Master said about the ordinary business of living from day to day? For these and similar reasons, with the change of emphasis from the clouds to the all too solid earth, written gospels had become a necessity.

It would go far beyond the scope of this book to embark upon the fascinating study of the varying character of the four gospels, reflecting the special interests of their authors and the particular purpose they had in mind in compiling them. Something must be said, however, of the relationships between

37

them and of their respective reliability as evidence for the life
and teaching of Jesus.

The whole Bible is the record of the revelation of what God
is like, of what He has done and still does for the world and
mankind. All this is transmitted through the imperfect medium
of the human minds of prophets and priests, apostles and
evangelists, to say nothing of scribes. Verbal infallibility is
thus out of the question. By the same token we cannot expect
any providential intervention in the case of the gospels to
ensure their accuracy even although they are our main source
for any knowledge of the historical Jesus.

We can never say with scientific certainty of a saying or an
incident in the gospels: This is precisely how such a thing
happened, or, These without a shadow of doubt are the very
words Jesus used. We must make allowance for the human
factor, remembering that as the essence of the Christian faith
is that God came to men in the human form of Jesus, with all
the limitations that this involves, so it is through the very
human minds of the men who knew Jesus that we get any
picture of how He lived and what He said. For example, a
saying of Jesus in St. John's gospel need have no less historical
value than a saying in St. Mark's gospel, even if it transpires
that the one is the kind of thing that a devout early Christian
believed that Jesus had meant, while the other is almost certainly what He did say. On the other hand, if we can show
that some parts of the gospels are for various reasons closer
to Jesus in time and origin than other parts, we shall feel more
confident that we have come as near to the actual words and
deeds of the Jesus who trod the earth as we can ever hope to
do.

The Synoptic Problem

The outstanding impression left on any reader of the four
gospels is the difference between the Gospel according to St.
John and the other three. The one feature that seems more or
less the same in all four is the Passion narrative, but apart from

that St. John seems to have selected different incidents; Jesus talks in a different manner, and His ministry centres mostly in Jerusalem instead of in Galilee. Having noted that, the next impression left is how closely the first three gospels agree. The general scheme of Jesus' ministry is the same in Matthew, Mark and Luke and, more remarkable than that, the wording is in many cases identical (e.g. Matt. 9. 6; Luke 5. 24). Jesus spoke Aramaic, not Greek, yet His recorded sayings turn out to be often exactly alike when they appear in these three Greek documents. On the other hand, in what would appear to be matters of considerable importance, e.g. the Nativity and Passion stories, there may be quite a large amount of variation.

This problem of the similarities and differences between the first three, or synoptic,gospels has exercised critical minds since the second century. We must confine ourselves here to the solution which commends itself most to modern scholarship as the best we can do with a highly complex issue. To state it thus so bluntly is by no means to suggest that further evidence or discoveries may not necessitate some modification. It is, however, on the whole a reasonably probable answer based on sound scientific methods.

It would seem clear from the evidence that two documents were in existence earlier than Luke or Matthew, and that they were used by both of them. One of these documents was our present gospel of Mark or a slightly different edition of it, and the other document was one containing largely the teaching of Jesus, called Q for convenience. Thus both Matthew and Luke made up their gospels by combining Mark and Q. But in addition to using Mark and Q both Matthew and Luke had at their disposal other material concerning Jesus, presumably not in written form, which was current in the particular Christian communities in which they wrote.

This would account for the fact that out of about 660 verses in Mark about 610 of them are to be found in Matthew or Luke or both. It is clear from the way Matthew and Luke try to improve on Mark, by correcting his grammar and phrasing, and by eliminating possible misunderstandings, that it was they who copied from Mark and not vice versa. Further, both Matthew and Luke have in common more than 200 verses, principally consisting of the teaching of Jesus, which are not found in Mark, and which must have come from an independent collection of sayings, presumably used by the missionaries in their campaigns, which for want of a better name is called Q.

The reason for saying that Matthew had some additional source of his own is that his gospel has a number of parables, incidents and sayings which are found nowhere else in the gospels. It is most natural to think that these were current traditions in Christian circles in which the author moved. Similarly, the gospel of St. Luke has much in it that is peculiar to that gospel, including such well-known parables as the Good Samaritan and the Prodigal Son. We know from Acts 21. 8 that the writer of that book, who was also the author of the Third Gospel, stayed for some time in Caesarea about A.D. 59. It is therefore most likely that although he was not a native of Palestine he used the time at his disposal there to collect local traditions about Jesus which he later included in his gospel. He may even have made an early draft of his gospel, consisting of what he gleaned in Palestine together with Q, which he expanded in due course by including extracts from Mark when that gospel came into his hands.

Mark

What do we know of the four writers of the gospels, their purpose in writing and their methods, and more particularly their contact with the events they describe? Tradition from Papias onwards, and he is quoting from the Presbyter John who was contemporary with Mark, is unanimous that the author of the gospel which stands second in the New Testament was the John Mark who first appears in Acts 12. 12. He was the son of the Mary in whose house in Jerusalem the first

Christians met after the Resurrection, in the 'upper room' of which, perhaps, the Last Supper was held.

If this was so, not only might Mark have been the "man bearing a pitcher of water" who led the disciples to that secret tryst (Mark 14. 13), but also, and more certainly, the young man who evaded the Temple police when Jesus was arrested in the Garden of Gethsemane (Mark 14. 51–52). His close association with St. Paul is written into the book of Acts, but more important in view of Papias' testimony is St. Peter's reference to him as "my son" (1 Pet. 5. 13)—presumably Mark was one of his converts—when he is writing from Rome. Since Mark was with St. Peter then he would have ample opportunity to learn at first hand from the leader of the Twelve details of Jesus' work and words which only one of the inner circle of the disciples could provide. Doubtless it was this authority of St. Peter behind Mark's gospel that made the other evangelists so ready to incorporate Mark's material in their own books.

In all probability St. Mark wrote his gospel in Rome after St. Peter's martyrdom, to preserve his teaching for the benefit of the little church there and to strengthen them in their resistance to Nero's violent persecution. No one bearing in mind the association of St. Peter and St. Mark can fail to detect on every page of the gospel the authentic note of an eyewitness. It is not merely vividness of description but the countless small details which point to an actual spectator of the events in question.

We have the strongest grounds for saying that in this gospel we have access through St. Peter to the actual scenes in the life of Jesus in which he played a major role. We have also good grounds for thinking that St. Mark himself as a young man had been involved to some extent in the events of Passion Week, and, as we have seen, any member of the Church, to say nothing of the missionaries of which St. Mark was one, had a general idea of the outline of Jesus' ministry. We may assume that Q was already in circulation and that this gospel was

41

designed to supplement it as the 'action' part of Jesus' activity. So with the reminiscences of St. Peter and his own personal knowledge fitted into the original traditional outline of Jesus' life, St. Mark compiles this piece of evidence of paramount historical importance. It is our primary source for the works of Jesus.

Luke

For the words of Jesus we must turn to Matthew and Luke who reproduce His teaching based on the document Q. There is no reason however to imagine that Q contained all that Jesus ever said. Many of His sayings must have failed to find a place in this collection either because they were not understood or because they did not make a sufficient impression on the hearers. Moreover, even within the gospels there are many words of Jesus which are not common to Matthew and Luke, and therefore not identifiable as Q. But they are not for that reason necessarily less authentic.

The Third Gospel is best described as a Christian apologia to the pagan world. It is an attempt to show that the Gospel, far from being merely an affair of a small Jewish sect, is universal in its appeal, and that it is not a disruptive but an integrating factor in society. Its author was Luke, the "beloved physician" who accompanied St. Paul as a member of his missionary team. Although he himself was a Gentile convert, perhaps from Macedonia, he was in an excellent position not only from his two years's stay at Caesarea, but from his contacts with apostolic circles, to collect the valuable material for our knowledge of Jesus which is not found in either Mark or Q.

St. Mark's style is notoriously rough and unpolished. St. Luke's gospel is on the other hand of high literary quality and his work is that of a careful scholar and skilful historian. His broad humanity and wide sympathies lead him to emphasize features in the life of Jesus which are of inestimable value when we try to arrive at a true picture of Christ. It is in these pages more than anywhere else in the gospels that we see Jesus breaking down the barriers of race and class, as a man of boundless compassion and constant prayer.

The gospel as we have it dates from between A.D. 70–80, drawing on Mark and Q and St. Luke's own considerable contribution, together with the infancy stories in the first two chapters, obviously derived from old Jewish–Christian tradition. All of this is of outstanding importance for our study of the life of Jesus. But if those scholars are right who argue for an early draft of the gospel (Proto-Luke) dating from about A.D. 60, i.e. before Mark, we are brought even nearer in time to the events of our Lord's ministry.

Matthew

Less reliance can be placed on the Gospel according to St. Matthew, although it was for centuries more highly esteemed than Mark. It is easy to see why. It forms the obvious bridge between the Old Testament and the New, hence its position as the first gospel. It has a more Jewish flavour than any other gospel and its author's main purpose is to show how all the hopes and prayers of Israel have been fulfilled in Christ. He is the Messiah who has brought to birth the New Israel, no longer limited to one nation, but world-wide in its scope and purpose.

As it stands it cannot be the work of the St. Matthew who was one of the twelve disciples for it is in effect a revised and enlarged edition of Mark. No apostle who had been a member of Jesus' intimate circle would be content to describe incidents in His ministry in the exact words of another man who was at best a secondary witness. What obliges us to treat Matthew's picture of Jesus with some caution is, however, the fact that when he alters the form of a story which he takes from Mark it is generally in the direction of overlaying the human attributes of Jesus, which Mark so faithfully records, with a veneer of divinity.

The author of Matthew is primarily a zealous and devout

Christian teacher whose concern is that Mark's bluntness and realism should not mislead the faithful. So with the best intentions he amends or omits anything that seems to emphasize the human limitations of Jesus or the disciples and removes them that much further from the workaday world so clearly reproduced in Mark and Luke. In the narrative material peculiar to Matthew's gospel it is noteworthy how many of the incidents are miraculous and it is generally agreed that this particular element in the gospels is of least value in arriving at a true picture of Jesus' ministry. Some of the miracles in Matthew approach the borderline of the apocryphal gospels and serve mainly to show up more clearly the value of Mark and Luke.

On the other hand, as a repository of the teaching of Jesus, Matthew is very useful. Unlike St. Luke who intersperses the sayings of Jesus which he has taken from Q with the general narrative of the ministry, and no doubt preserves them in better chronological order, Matthew, with a passion for orderliness and a teacher's concern, groups the sayings of Jesus, whether they come from Q or elsewhere, in accordance with subject matter and in five great discourses, the best known of which is the Sermon on the Mount. The advantage of this is obvious when we try to get an overall impression of Jesus' teaching.

John

Lastly, the Fourth Gospel. What reliance can we place on a book which until quite recently was considered even by conservative critics to be a second century production? No one has ever doubted its theological or devotional value, or that the author, whoever he was, had, of all New Testament writers, the deepest insight into the mind of Christ. Even if we recognize that all the gospels are a mixture of history and interpretation, the element of interpretation in the Fourth Gospel seemed to be so great as to nullify its historical value.

Recent study and further evidence have combined to bring

44

about a remarkable change. Some scholars would now date the Fourth Gospel as early as Luke and earlier than Matthew and all would place it firmly within the first century. Although the authorship is far from settled, John the son of Zebedee, one of the twelve disciples, is now regarded as being much more closely connected with the gospel than was at one time thought to be the case. There is good ground for thinking that the relationship between the actual author and the old apostle is not unlike that between St. Peter and St. Mark.

While at one time it was thought that this was simply an anonymous product of a reflective Christian in Asia Minor, moderate opinion among scholars now inclines to see the author as a Jewish disciple of John the apostle, then an old man in Ephesus, who is in this gospel seeking to present Christ in an intelligible way to the non-Jewish world, but basing his presentation on the recollections of the old apostle about the Jesus he had known.

On examination of the differences between the Fourth Gospel and the synoptic gospels it transpires that they are more apparent than real, and that where they differ on points of fact John is as likely to be right as Mark. The two approaches are complementary rather than contradictory. The synoptic gospels give us a series of photographs of Jesus, the Fourth Gospel provides us with a portrait. In this sense it is the work of an artist rather than of a scientific historian but it is in that respect perhaps a truer picture of the life and times of Jesus, just as a good portrait does not catch merely the passing expression of a moment as does a photograph, but gathers the essence of the subject into one likeness.

There is no such thing as a Jesus of history as opposed to a Christ of faith. Every word that is written about Him in the New Testament or outside of it is a record of the impact He made upon men. If we say that the synoptic gospels record more nearly the local setting of the words of Jesus and incidents of His life, we must at the same time say that to understand what Jesus means we must set the Fourth Gospel

45

alongside the synoptics. St. John's purpose is to speak from faith to faith, to communicate to his readers what Christ had come to mean for him over the years, and we cannot get closer to the Jesus who walked and talked in Galilee and Judaea than by seeing Him through the eyes of "the disciple whom Jesus loved" (21. 20). When Jesus says: I am the Bread of Life, or the Good Shepherd, or the Light of the World, we not only can be sure that He said it but also that the Beloved Disciple had experienced it to be true.

This was plain to the early Church as far back as Clement of Alexandria who wrote: "Having observed that the bodily things had been exhibited in the other gospels, John, inspired by the Spirit, produced a spiritual gospel." The Fourth Gospel is the life of the historical Jesus seen *sub specie aeternitatis*. It seeks to make it clear to a later generation living far from Palestine that the Good News was not time- or place-conditioned, but that men and women who had never seen Jerusalem and cared nothing for Jewry, who lived in an altogether different world, could still become Christ's disciples and share that life in all its fullness. What made Christianity a world religion was, as much as anything, the presentation in the Fourth Gospel of what was best in Jewish thought in a form that was intellectually acceptable to educated pagan minds.

THE BACKGROUND

Chapter Four

PALESTINE AND THE PAGAN WORLD

The Roman Empire

BEFORE considering what the gospels tell us about the life and teaching of Jesus we ought to look first at the kind of world He lived in. The atmosphere of the gospels is so intensely Jewish that it is difficult to realize that Rome was mistress of the world. From the Atlantic to Arabia, from Britain to the Sahara there was a unity such as there had never been before. The frontiers were open; national antagonisms were in abeyance; old rivalries between states and petty warfare alike were suspended while a great peace—the *Pax Romana*—reigned over the whole world, certainly an enforced peace but none the less welcome.

Roman cohorts and legions, scattered throughout the length and breadth of the Mediterranean, preserved law and order not so much by strength of numbers as by the political power they represented. There was much in common between Roman and British imperialism. Both were amorphous growths, both had a genius for colonization, both had the great gift of tolerance. Thus the Roman authorities were content, so long as peace was maintained, to allow their subject peoples to adhere to their own customs, their own religion, their own political systems and their own tongues. When Gallio is said in Acts 18. 17 to have "cared for none of these things", namely Jewish religious disputes, it was not that he was indifferent to serious matters but that he was a good Roman official pursuing a policy of non-interference.

Augustus, grand-nephew of Julius Caesar, and first Roman emperor, under whose sovereignty Jesus was born (Luke 2. 1) was the real architect of this great organism, and though his

47

successors—such as Tiberius, Caligula, Claudius and Nero—
fell far short of his greatness and became latterly a byword
for incompetence and vicious practices, the empire they ruled
was the channel through which Christianity had to flow,
which determined the bounds of the new faith and which was
in turn revolutionized by it.

Rome followed the principle of delegation of authority to
the fullest possible extent. There was no attempt to centralize
government in the capital. If a conquered city or country had
a reasonably efficient administration it was encouraged to
continue. It was responsible for raising its own taxes, running
its own public services, issuing its own coinage and admin-
istering its own laws. Only when disorder or inefficiency pre-
vented this—as happened in Palestine—did the imperial
government step in and take control.

This left the individual as well as the community a large
amount of independence. He paid taxes indirectly to Rome
but in return he lived in a much more secure world than that
of his fathers. He was not obliged to do military service unless
in an emergency and all Jews were completely exempt. The
army was sufficiently attractive as a career to gain all the
recruits it wanted. Latin was not insisted on as the official
language since Greek was the *lingua franca* and native tongues
were not discouraged.

A man could move from one end of the empire to the other,
if he were so disposed, without restriction and in comparative
safety. Police and military protection was well organized in
districts known to harbour brigands. An excellent network of
imperial roads traversed the empire and inns were probably
no worse than in certain parts of Europe today. From the hills
near Nazareth Jesus could look down on such roads along
which passed a constant stream of traffic—merchants,
soldiers, officials, as well as the vast variety of pilgrims, scholars,
students and charlatans who travelled about the ancient
world.

The aristocracy of the empire was moneyed rather than

48

privileged and fortunes were made largely by the exploitation of conquered peoples. The middle class was separated by the proletariat—whose main concern was "bread and circuses"—from the lowest class of all, the slaves, who numbered half the population. This unwholesome phenomenon which had originated in a long series of conquests, each producing captives, varied considerably in character between the western and eastern parts of the empire. It was in the west that its cruelty was most apparent. There the slave gangs, mostly men from Gaul and Britain, were treated more like animals than men.

In the eastern Mediterranean zone, however, slavery was a comparatively mild institution, organized on a domestic basis, with the possibility of buying freedom and opportunities for subsequent advancement in the state. It is perhaps for this reason that Jesus, like St. Paul, had nothing to say in condemnation of it as an institution. A slave had generally a better life than a hired man.

Greek Culture

While Rome provided the government of the empire, maintained the peace and administered justice, it was nevertheless in essence still the empire which Alexander the Great had founded, Greek in character if Roman in name. Rome's predecessor as the great world power, although now subject to her new rulers, dominated their lives in everything except political and military power. Captured Greece had taken captive warrior Rome.

Educated Romans vied with each other in demonstrating their devotion to anything that was Greek. The highest art of the Augustan age was to imitate the great Greek masters and the whole structure of the civilized life of the empire was built on the Greek pattern. Especially was this true in the matter of language. The Greek of Athens had become the basis of a common tongue which was now within the empire the normal means of communication between foreigners from

Rome to India and round practically the whole of the Mediterranean coast.

Common Greek—or Koiné—was the second language of those who spoke Latin, Aramaic or whatever the local tongue might be. Thus although Jesus and the disciples spoke Aramaic—the everyday language as opposed to the classical Hebrew of the Scriptures—when the gospels came to be written down the obvious medium of communication was Greek. Later when St. Paul was writing to Romans or Asians, Macedonians or Achaians, he had at his disposal a language which was as readily understood by the one as by the other.

It is worth remembering too that another result of the spread of Greek culture was that Christianity came into an educated world—into a world of sophisticated cities, equipped with schools and universities, where men discussed continually the very questions that Christianity professed to answer. Though it had its birth on the pastoral slopes of the Galilean hills it was in the cities of the Graeco-Roman world that it took root—foreign cities hundreds of miles away from Athens but places where an old Athenian might well have felt at home amid the temples and colonnades, theatres and gymnasia, where men wore Greek clothes, spoke the Greek language and aped Greek manners.

It belongs more to the next stage of the spread of the Christian faith than to the period when Jesus lived and worked in Galilee, to consider how the breakdown of ancient pagan religion and its replacement by the mystery religions and the morality of the philosophers paved the way for the spread of Christianity. By the same token the existence of Jewish communities scattered throughout the empire was to form the bridge between the Palestinian origin of the gospel and its impact upon the pagan world. Devout Gentiles, dissatisfied with the mythology of Olympus and disturbed by the breakdown of ordinary behaviour, found in the synagogues of the Jews of the Dispersion an oasis of stability, of respect for high moral standards, of a wholesome family life, and a legacy of law, prophecy, psalmody and wisdom which commanded respect and invited assent.

Jewish Exclusiveness

The fact remains that despite the conditions that obtained in the world at large, Palestine at this point in history might almost have been living in a different age. It was nominally part of the Roman empire but as we can see from the gospels the outside world impinged but little on the self-contained Jewish community in the Levant. Pontius Pilate and the Roman soldiers play their part but it is a peripheral, albeit momentous role. Galilee may be 'Galilee of the Gentiles', foreign trade may pass up and down the caravan routes not far from Nazareth, Tiberias the capital on the Lake of Galilee may be a wholly Greek city, and the ten cities of the Decapolis a Gentile enclave, but the evidence of the gospels is that Jesus and His followers were Jews by birth and conviction, children of the Old Testament heritage, and highly conscious of the unique part that Israel was destined to play in God's providential ordering of human affairs.

It would be in keeping with modern taste to think that Jesus and the disciples were by virtue of their upbringing in a more cosmopolitan part of Palestine than the rigid self-contained isolationism of Jerusalem, conditioned to become citizens of the world. There is no evidence to support this view. Jesus mixed with Gentiles, outcasts and the other victims of the policies of apartheid in the ancient world because He believed in the Fatherhood of God and not because He was a citizen of a world-wide empire. His disciples followed His example for no other reason than that the prodding of the Holy Spirit of God left them no alternative.

The world into which Jesus came was therefore essentially a small world. The three main counties—for a large county is about their modern equivalent—moving from north to south, were Galilee, Samaria and Judaea. The other districts mentioned in Luke 3. 1 play no important part in the record. All in all the whole area was no bigger than Wales. From the coastal plain on the edge of the Mediterranean, through the foothills to the central mountain ridge, then down to the Jordan valley, the country presents geographical and climatic features without parallel on this planet. Mt. Hermon is over 9,000 feet high; the Dead Sea at the end of the Jordan's course is 1,300 feet below sea level. Yet the whole country is not more than 150 miles in length and about 50 miles across.

The climatic as well as the territorial differences have led to the development of a self-contained people. Israel may for centuries have been a pawn in the game of world politics because of her vulnerable position on the route from Mesopotamia to Egypt, but by the same token by virtue of her relative inaccessibility among the hills she could preserve her identity and her traditions without great difficulty. This is in effect what happened and in order to understand the gospels properly we must go back to about two hundred years before Jesus was born.

By that time Alexander the Great had left as his legacy a world-empire which was dominated by Greek manners and Greek thought. Lesser men, among whom his empire had been divided, were seized with a mission to inculcate Greek civilization into the Mediterranean world. Not least among these was Antiochus IV of Syria, into whose domains Palestine was incorporated.

Having tried in vain by gentle means to persuade the Jews that Greek culture meant progress and enlightenment, Antiochus felt himself compelled to take strong measures. In 168 B.C. he ordered an altar to be set up in the Temple at Jerusalem to the pagan god Zeus; the priests were commanded to sacrifice swine and to drink the broth in defiance of the Law of Moses; the Old Testament scriptures were to be publicly burned and circumcision was to be summarily abolished.

Whatever sympathies some of the more liberal Jews may have had with this progressive policy of modernism, such a violation of ancient law and tradition could not be condoned.

Rebellion broke out under the leadership of a family of brothers, the Maccabees, and the Jewish War of Independence had begun. Within two years the rebels had cleared the enemy out of the land; the Temple was rededicated and the independent kingdom of the Maccabeans was inaugurated. Although it ended in a dynastic struggle for power between the rival factions of the family, the memory of Judas Maccabaeus was not readily forgotten, nor the hope of a similar overthrow of Roman power when she succeeded Greece as mistress of the world.

Political Developments

As it happened Rome entered Jerusalem in the first instance by invitation and not by conquest. The Jewish people were weary of misgovernment by the later Maccabean kings and in desperation in 63 B.C. they encouraged Roman intervention to settle a disputed succession to the throne. Pompey, the Roman general who was in the Near East at the time, went to Jerusalem ostensibly to arbitrate but in effect to bring Judaea under the Roman eagle. From then on through the lifetime of Jesus until the final clash of A.D. 66–70 which ended in the Fall of Jerusalem and the devastation of the whole country, the Jews were subject to the authority of Rome.

When Jesus was born, Palestine was a monarchy by permission of the Emperor Augustus. Its ruler was Herod the Great who has been given this classic description by Bishop Gore: Edomite by birth, Jew by religion, Greek by sympathies and Roman by allegiance. This extraordinary man tried to combine patronage of paganism and Judaism in an atmosphere of lordly magnificence. He built new Greek cities and pagan temples throughout the land, and a theatre and amphitheatre for gladiatorial shows and athletic games outside the walls of Jerusalem. His own palace there, brand new and glistening in marble and gold, became a centre of Greek culture.

Naturally, the orthodox Jews, who apart from any other considerations hated all Edomites on principle as the ancient enemies of Israel, viewed these developments with grave disfavour. On the other hand they could not but welcome the fact that Herod at the same time gave them every encouragement to carry on their own religious affairs as they wished. In addition he rebuilt the Temple at Jerusalem to make it one of the wonders of the world. Construction was still in progress in the lifetime of Jesus (Mark 13. 1; John 2. 20), but general satisfaction was diminished by the fact that Herod insisted on putting a Roman eagle above the great door and imposing heavy taxation to finance the project.

The Pharisees refused to take an oath of loyalty to Herod as king and adopted an attitude of non-cooperation rather than of open hostility. Perhaps wholesale revolt would not have been easy in view of the chain of fortresses which Herod maintained throughout the land and which he manned with foreign mercenaries. It was in one of these castles, Machaerus, east of the Dead Sea that John the Baptist is said to have met his end. Herod's latter days were clouded with madness and crime, and he died just at the change of the eras in 4 B.C.

In a sense he was a second Solomon in his expensive tastes and polygamous habits, but unlike Solomon's reign his term of office was looked back on with loathing. Some thought that his rule had been better than that of a Roman governor, but it had been a reign of terror. Crucifixions, burnings and massacres had been common practice. After his death the Jews sent a special mission to Rome to plead with the emperor to take the country under his direct protection and have done with Herod and his house. Augustus, however, would not agree.

The land was divided among the three sons of Herod. Archelaus became Ethnarch of Judaea, Antipas became Tetrarch of Galilee, and Philip, Tetrarch of the north-east. Philip was the best of the trio and is chiefly known for his building of Caesarea Philippi (Mark 8. 27). Herod Antipas, the Herod of the gospels, built the city of Tiberias, the capital of Galilee, but is probably better known from the fact that his bigamous marriage to the notorious Herodias provoked the indignation of John the Baptist and led to the latter's murder after the famous banquet at which Salome danced (Mark 6. 17–28).

The ethnarchy of Judaea was obviously the most important of the three offices and Archelaus was as it happened the worst of Herod's sons. His reign of ten years, 4 B.C.–A.D. 6, was inaugurated with rioting and continued in rebellions and massacres. At last the emperor acceded to popular demand and Judaea was put under the direct control of Roman procuraators, responsible to the legate of the province of Syria, and through him to the emperor himself.

In the Roman system of imperial government a procurator was not a dignitary of great consequence. His function generally was to manage the emperor's estates in the various provinces. Only in a few colonies of a more backward character was a procurator considered to be sufficiently important to act as governor. Judaea was reckoned to come into this category. So while Herod Antipas and Philip continued to govern the north, the south came under the authority of a succession of these minor Roman officials.

Normally they lived at Caesarea, on the coast, but on special occasions, such as religious festivals, they came to Jerusalem to deal with any disturbance that might occur. To assist them to keep order they had a small force of a few thousand soldiers scattered about the country. Pontius Pilate was the fifth of these procurators. He was appointed in A.D. 26. His reputation among his contemporaries was that of a merciless soldier who kept the people quiet by dint of brutal repression. Eventually the legate of Syria, Vitellius, thought Pilate had gone too far and he was sent back to Rome to face a charge of massacring civilians without adequate reason. There he was found guilty and was banished to Gaul.

There was a brief change of government when Herod Agrippa, grandson of Herod the Great, became king by Roman permission not only of Judaea but of Galilee and the north-eastern territories. On his death in A.D. 44, however, the system of procurators was restored and the whole of Palestine became a Roman province. The last years before the Fall of Jerusalem were marked by a series of bad procurators and by increasingly strained relations between the Jews and the Roman authorities. Lawlessness became rampant, riots became chronic, patriots were crucified in great numbers; robbery, murder and corruption were universal.

At length in A.D. 66 it came to open rebellion which spread throughout the land. For four years the Romans tried to restore order and there was bitter fighting as well as civil strife among the Jews themselves. Jerusalem was besieged and finally captured. The last months of the siege had been months of acute misery. Only a handful of fanatical defenders remained when in A.D. 70 the Temple was stormed and burned. The conqueror Titus ransacked the Temple treasures, and his triumphal arch with carvings of the seven-branched candlestick and the table of the bread of the Presence can still be seen in the Forum at Rome. So many had been killed and taken prisoner that a mere remnant was left to exist among the ruins of Jerusalem and the other devastated cities.

Chapter Five

ROMANS AND JEWS

Roman Oppression

THE noteworthy feature of this whole period is obviously the increasingly chaotic situation leading to inevitable disaster. Revolts, riots and war could have only one outcome when the antagonists were so ill-matched: on the one hand a mighty empire, on the other, a handful of enthusiasts. Unlike the days of the Maccabees the Jews were now up against a solid imperial military power which through sheer weight of numbers was bound to crush them. In the fifty years before the end of the old era and the first fifty years of the new, there was not a year that passed in Palestine without bloodshed.

The *Pax Romana* which lay like a benevolent pall over the rest of the world did not extend to the Holy Land. There alone there was violence, tumult and sudden death. Sporadic reigns of terror, constant repression, spying and cruelty sapped the courage of the stoutest hearts. It is little wonder that the pages of the gospels are studded with so many victims of mental disorders and disease. The root of the matter was that the Jews did not understand the Romans and the Romans did not understand the Jews.

Imperial Rome was on the whole not a bad mistress of her subject peoples. She gave them peace, religious toleration and justice, and no man needed a passport. If there was ground for complaint it lay in the charge that has been levelled at the British in India and elsewhere, namely a lack of sensitivity and a failure to understand, or to try to understand, that there might be more things in the minds of colonial peoples than a desire to eat adequately, to sleep comfortably and to leave the rest to the ruling power.

The Jews were the Romans' greatest thorn in the flesh. It

was understandable that they should rebel against the heavy taxation. So did other colonies. It was also normal that they should hope for independence and try to achieve it. But that they should treat as a matter of life and death harmless symbols like the image of the emperor, or theatres and athletic stadia, or the use of Temple monies to build an aqueduct— this was beyond Roman comprehension.

What Roman could understand the mentality of people who in the year A.D. 40 when the Emperor Caligula wished to set up an image of himself as a god in the Temple, flocked to the Roman legate in their thousands, leaving their homes and fields, prostrated themselves on the ground, bared their necks and asked to be killed rather than permit such sacrilege? Naturally the Roman mind, unable to comprehend this religious mania, employed stronger and sterner methods of dealing with these obdurate fanatics. They in their turn, at least those capable of fighting, mostly preferred guerrilla warfare to passive resistance.

Messianism

The more severe the Roman measures became against them, the more highly coloured became the Jews' expectation that the Messiah was at hand. The numerous rebellions were led by men who not only wanted secular freedom but who fought with religious fanaticism in the belief that they were hastening the Messiah's coming. The caricature of the typical Hebrew as primarily a financial manipulator has nothing in common with these passionate visionaries, in deadly earnest about their convictions and prepared to give their lives for them.

The expectation of a coming Messiah was deeply rooted in Israel's past. Psalmists and prophets had voiced the hope that one day God would show His hand. Convinced as they were that the chances and changes of history were overruled by divine Providence, they could not believe that their faith in the ultimate victory of good over evil was mistaken. They had had signal evidence in the life of their own nation that the

Creator of the world and Lord of all nations had destined Israel for a special role, namely to be His witnesses and advocates among the peoples who lived in ignorance of His purpose to bring all mankind into the right relationship to Himself and to each other.

If at times this role of Israel as mediator between God and the nations of the world was sometimes seen in terms of nationalistic self-assertion, the best thought of the Old Testament had always seen Israel's vocation as essentially lying in the field of religion and morality. It was to be their mission to set a standard in public and private life of such moral excellence and religious conviction that in God's good time a new era would dawn where peace and righteousness, truth and mercy would replace the injustice and hatred, ruthlessness and oppression which dominated the world as they knew it.

As these hopes and aspirations took shape so did the concept of a human agent, set apart by God as His anointed representative, to bring this new age into being. He would be a second David, the king who above all the rest had moved the hearts and minds of his people, had himself embodied piety and resolution, a true son of the best Israelite traditions, and the creator of what in retrospect seemed to be the Golden Age of Israel's chequered story. Yet even in its early stages this belief in the new age that would one day dawn and the Messiah who would be instrumental in bringing it about had an element of the supernatural about it.

Messiah might be a son of David but he would be no ordinary king. Isaiah's picture of the divinely appointed Deliverer has already overtones of more than human attributes. He will be the Wonderful Counsellor, Mighty God, Everlasting Father and Prince of Peace (Isa. 9. 6). It is thus not surprising that as political events propelled Israel into an ever-darkening world where the powers of paganism and militarism seemed to be in the ascendant, the hope of any betterment of the present world should have given place to the conviction that God could do nothing with this present corruption, and that

59

only an end of the existing order in cataclysm and disintegration could pave the way for the advent of the Messiah as a supernatural figure sent from God to reign over a new heaven and a new earth.

These two conflicting concepts of the Messiah, as a political deliverer on the one hand, and as a supernatural visitant from heaven, provide the background for the situation which obtained in the time of Jesus. John the Baptist, as we shall see, was the outstanding representative of those who were looking for one who would bring the existing order to an end and usher in a new era. In the popular mind, however, the Messiah was quite clearly a political figure who might appear at any time and whose first act would be to destroy the Romans and restore the glory of Israel. Whatever form this expectation took, people were prepared, according to Klausner, "to see in every wonder-worker and preacher a prospective saviour and ruler, a king and Messiah, a supernatural political saviour and a spiritual saviour filled with the divine spirit."[1]

Economic Conditions

The social and economic conditions of the people about this time seem to have encouraged the general unrest and atmosphere of expectancy. Though most trades were practised and fishing was the staple industry of Galilee, Palestine was predominantly a land of smallholders, who like smallholders everywhere lived a hand-to-mouth existence. A year or two of bad harvests were enough to put them in the hands of the moneylenders (the 'adversary' of Matt. 5.25) or condemn them to servitude. Their sons would become either beggars or brigands.

Men of property were comparatively few, and men without any land at all who hired themselves out as labourers were plentiful. So in this ill-balanced society with a large impoverished proletariat, whenever unemployment set in, which was frequently, there was ample material for unrest and discontent. Such men together with the slave-class were behind the

[1] *Jesus of Nazareth*, p. 201.

numerous rebellions and religious movements of the period.

Taxation too was a crushing burden. The Maccabeans had pursued a healthy economic policy: Herod the Great had done the reverse. His extravagant building schemes had left a legacy of debt and necessitated taxation which seemed beyond endurance. The Roman procurators, however, out-Heroded Herod. Their tax collectors or *publicani* became another name for robbers, ruffians and reprobates. The gospels bracket 'publicans' with sinners.

There were water taxes, city taxes, meat and salt taxes, road taxes and house taxes. Pliny says that "at every stopping-place by land or sea some tax was levied". When in addition to this taxation there was the extortion of the collectors to whom the taxes were farmed out the situation became intolerable. The reaction of the more robust elements in Palestine was to revolt against Rome and that of the more helpless elements was to wait and pray for the speedy coming of the Messiah.

A major part in the background of the life of Jesus is played by the religious parties in the Jewish community. In reality these factions were legion, shading off into one another, nor can they properly be described as being concerned only with religion, since politics and religion were inextricably bound up together. But on broad lines, as the gospels indicate, the division into Pharisees, mostly laymen, and Sadducees, who were priests, was generally accepted.

The Pharisees

The extreme left wing of the Pharisaic party was known as the zealots. One of them became a disciple of Jesus (Luke 6. 15). These young enthusiasts were less concerned about religion than about political freedom. They conducted guerrilla warfare against the Romans or Herod as the case might be, and included the well-to-do among their enemies. They were generally called 'robbers' by the respectable members of the community who deplored their revolutionary tactics, and as often as not ended on a cross like the two who were crucified at the same time as Jesus.

At the other extreme were the Essenes, a monastic order for men and women with various settlements throughout Palestine. Their practices were ascetic, they were self-supporting, and wore a distinctive white dress. Though they are not mentioned in the New Testament and though there is no evidence to prove that John the Baptist was ever a member of one of these communities, it is not impossible, since his outlook was not dissimilar. Jesus' attitude to the world and to people, however, could not have been more different from what is known about the habits of such an Essene community as that of Qumran which came to light through the discovery of their library, now world-famous as the Dead Sea Scrolls.

The main body of the Pharisees, however, avoided extremes. They were the popular middle-class party, democratic in outlook and patriotic in spirit. Strong in their devotion to the terms of the Law of Moses, they earned the condemnation of Jesus because they adhered equally strongly to the traditional interpretation of the Law which expanded its provisions to cover every contingency. Thus with every detail of daily life regulated and controlled it had come to mean as much to fail to observe the Sabbath as to ill-treat a slave.

The Pharisees centred their attention on the synagogues rather than on the Temple. They tended to leave the Temple and its ritual to the Sadducees, and to concentrate on translating religion into terms of daily life. Though they hated the Romans they were not prepared to make it a political issue. Confident that the Messiah would come in God's own time they were content to leave things in His hands so long as they were allowed to practise their religion in peace. In this central bloc were no doubt such families as that of Joseph of Nazareth and Simeon and Anna of Jerusalem (Luke 2. 25–38). Such were the quiet folk in the land, pious, law-abiding, expectant; taking no part in politics at all, sympathizing naturally with all patriots, but basing their hopes more on the coming of the Messiah as the solution to all their troubles.

The Sadducees

The wealthy, aristocratic Sadducees were little loved. Their history went back to Maccabean times as did that of the Pharisees. But while the Pharisees had been then as later staunch upholders of Israelite faith and tradition, the Sadducees had first been identified with the 'progressive' attempts of Israel's foreign overlords to abolish the distinctive Jewish way of life and later had earned the reputation of subservience to the corrupt ruling house. People still felt that they were more concerned to feather their own nests than to work for the good of the community.

They took a narrower view of the Law than did the Pharisees. Only what was written in the five books of Moses was admitted by them to be valid or binding. Thus they did not believe in the doctrine of a general resurrection of the dead or in a hierarchy of angels (Acts 23. 8) since these beliefs did not bear the hallmark of antiquity. Most of all they deplored any references to a coming Messiah, who might disturb their happy relations with the Romans. The High Priests who were appointed by Rome as the chief executives of the Jewish state under the procurators were of course Sadducees. The most notable of them in these times was Annas who held office from A.D. 6–15, and after him his son-in-law Caiaphas who ruled from A.D. 18–36.

Under the High Priests, authority in the state was vested in the Sanhedrin, a general assembly consisting mostly of Sadducean priests, known in the gospels as the 'chief priests'. In addition there were the 'scribes', lawyers belonging mostly to the Pharisees, and elders, who were men of social standing in the community. Matters which could not be settled by local tribunals were referred to the Sanhedrin, but of course in the last resort Roman authority was supreme.

The Faith of Israel

Any attempt to paint a picture of the kind of world into which Jesus was born would be incomplete without some reference to the religious background which He inherited. He was a child of the Old Testament faith, and there is nothing more impressive in the religion and philosophy of the ancient world than the legacy of the priests, prophets, psalmists and wisdom scribes of Israel which every Jewish boy was heir to. If the thirty-first chapter of the book of Job may be taken as the standard of behaviour which was expected of a devout Jew around 400 B.C. it was not only one of which any nation might be proud in any age, but it is also a mark of the depth to which the message of the prophets of Israel had penetrated everyday life.

In the long story of Israel's increasing understanding of the nature and purpose of God, the prophets made a contribution which revolutionized religious thinking and changed the face of Israelite society. From their day on religion could no longer be divorced from morality. Piety and behaviour must be seen as two sides of the same coin. Attendance at religious festivals and performance of ritual were thenceforth meaningless unless they were seen in the context of total obedience to the will of God, which included day to day observance of justice, charity and personal integrity.

The God who revealed Himself to Israel through them was no capricious oriental potentate but the sole Power who held the universe in His hands, guided the destinies of nations and the lives of all His creatures. His ways were sometimes beyond man's understanding but His purposes were consistently governed by His love for men. Mercy rather than stern justice governed His actions and forgiveness was assured to all who turned to Him in penitence. Man's wayward and rebellious spirit which had been his undoing since Adam must be made to recognize the supreme authority of God over the whole of life.

The Law had been given to Moses as the pattern of behaviour expected of a people singled out from the rest of the nations to enter into a special covenant-relationship with God. Though He was Lord of all and though all men were in His care, He was in a peculiarly intimate sense the Israelites' God as they were in the same sense His chosen people. But they were chosen for service and not for favour. Their responsibility

64

was the greater, as was their accountability for failure, since this notable privilege had been conferred upon them.

The religion in which Jesus was brought up was thus primarily a religion of revelation. What Israel had been taught about God through Moses and the prophets was not the result of her unaided quest for truth, any more than her selection to be the People of God had been in any sense dependent on her own merits or her own achievements. It was a wonder and a mystery for which there could only be grateful acceptance and thankfulness. God had signally blessed Israel, despite her many failures for which she had been disciplined and chastened. Over the centuries she had learned that her role was not to be that of the great Gentile nations, but rather to be a light in their darkness, an oasis of truth in an erring world, a living witness to the presence of the living God among His creatures.

So the Temple at Jerusalem was like no other shrine on earth. It was there that the one true God was worshipped, where the ancient festivals were commemorated reminding His people as at Passover of His initial choice of Israel to be His people, or as at Pentecost of His revelation of the Law to Moses. In every village the synagogue was the centre of community life, where the children were schooled in the faith, where the Law and the prophets were read and expounded, where psalms were sung to the glory of God, where a liturgy was said of adoration, confession, thanksgiving and intercession, and from where prayer was carried into the homes of the people as the framework of daily life.

The great institution of the Sabbath, as a day when men rested from their everyday affairs and devoted themselves to worship and recollection, was a jealously guarded privilege observed by all Jews everywhere. Similarly circumcision as an outward sign of inward dedication and as a mark of membership of the people of God was a traditional practice which united all Jews in the spiritual kinship of a world-wide family.

It is easy to see how in the hands of fallible mortals such a faith could be travestied—how nationalistic pride could take the place of the prophetic idea of a people chosen for service; how self-righteousness could follow on punctilious observance of the Law; how the stone and mortar of Jerusalem and its Temple could become an object of worship instead of the God they existed to proclaim; how the Sabbath could become a nightmare of restrictions and circumcision a racial fetish. All these things did in fact happen.

Moreover it is certain that in the time of Jesus as in the time of the prophets this high faith and high morality left many people largely untouched. Then as now self-interest and apathy, greed and irresponsibility were more in evidence than moral excellence and private piety. But for those like Jesus who regarded religion as a matter of life and death, who were prepared to centre their lives on God and His service, to be born a Jew in Palestine at that time was to be given the opportunity to enter into a rich and moving heritage bequeathed by men who had themselves lived in the presence of God and had been shown something of the unimaginable mystery and glory of His Being.

This splendid legacy of Old Testament faith and morality is of much more importance when we attempt to assess the impact of Jesus upon His contemporaries and His significance for the world at large than some of the ideas that had been superimposed upon it in the period that intervened between the latest writings of the Hebrew scriptures and the birth of Jesus. It was in these years, as reflected in the books of the Apocrypha and even more in those writings which were not admitted to be authoritative, that the picture emerged of Satan and his demons as responsible for all the ills of mankind, and of a hierarchy of angelic beings, as intermediaries between God and man, framed in a hotch-potch of bizarre speculation about the end of the world. Although this too was part of Jesus' religious heritage it was not, as we shall see, of the essence of His message.

66

Chapter Six

THE RESURRECTION
FACT OR FANTASY?

I T is not theological obscurantism that suggests the Resurrection as the proper starting point for a life of Jesus. In fact it is a better place to begin than in the carpenter's shop at Nazareth. For if it is true that all that is recorded about Jesus in the gospels is written by men for whom the Resurrection was the supreme moment of illumination as to the true significance of Jesus, we shall not get our own perspective right in the matter of judging the historicity or otherwise of the gospel narratives until we are satisfied that the Resurrection itself, which the Bible claims to be the greatest miracle of all time, is founded on fact and not on fantasy.

The early Christians had no doubt that this was the crucial issue for belief. St. Paul states the case succinctly when he says: "If Christ has not been raised, then our preaching is in vain and your faith is in vain" (1 Cor. 15. 14). This is equally true today. If the Resurrection is a myth there is no reason to suppose that other extraordinary events reported in the gospels are anything more. If on the other hand the Resurrection story is true, we are given a yardstick by which to judge incidents and sayings of Jesus which would otherwise be open to suspicion as pious inventions.

This does not by any means imply that if we accept the Resurrection as a fact we should thereafter suspend our critical faculties in dealing with the gospel narratives. It does, however, suggest that we should exercise extreme caution in dismissing what are in effect much less unusual happenings in the course of Jesus' ministry. A prophet or a saint who is reported to have done and said normally incredible things but whose life ends in the normal way is in a different category from someone of whom the same type of extraordinary utterances and actions is reported but whose death has a unique sequel.

If the first Christians had not believed that Christ rose from the dead there would have been no Church and no New Testament. By the same token neither would there have been a Christendom nor a Western civilization. Such characteristic features of the modern world as the emancipation of women, the abolition of slavery, universal education, public care of the sick and infirm, provision of welfare services for the old and young, are the direct products of Christianity. They might well have come in other ways and under different auspices, but if we are dealing with facts and not with might-have-beens we must recognize that these and other social reforms have come about primarily because a group of Jews two thousand years ago became convinced that Jesus of Nazareth had risen from the dead.

If Christianity had been founded merely on the moral teaching of Jesus it would no doubt have flourished for a short time as a well-meaning deviation from orthodox Judaism. It would quickly have lost its identity amid the innumerable varieties of religion and philosophy which occupied the minds of the ancient world. Fine distinctions of religious belief such as that between Jews and Christians did not impress the matter-of-fact administrators of the Roman Empire. For them both brands of religion were equally eccentric. But although many of the first Christians might have been tempted by virtue of their Jewish background to subscribe to the official view that Jews and Christians were basically of one faith, they could not finally accept this identification because of their belief in the Resurrection.

It was certainly not because they were Jews that they had come to believe that their Master had conquered death. Indeed they had great difficulty in finding Old Testament texts to substantiate their conviction that Christ had risen (e.g. Matt. 12. 40; Acts 2. 25–27). Nor can we account for the Resurrection-faith by evidencing the existence of belief in dying and rising gods among the devotees of Hellenistic mystery-religions, which might have infiltrated into Christianity. Apart from the fact that the traffic may equally well have been in the opposite direction no mystery-cult ever claimed to be founded on a historical event. The myth of the dying and rising god was everywhere recognized to be based on the annual death and rebirth of vegetation in winter and spring. No more can we attribute the conviction of the first Christians that Christ had risen to some kind of wish-fulfilment. They were not expecting the Resurrection, and, when it happened, they dismissed the report of it as 'an idle tale' (Luke 24. 11).

The Resurrection Faith

So let us go back to the first Good Friday, the day of the Crucifixion. There we encounter a band of men and women who had been brought together by their common devotion to a Master whom they revered as a teacher, who spoke with unique authority and who healed the sick with startling success. For a variety of reasons they had been drawn to this strange and enigmatic figure by the power of His personality, by what He said and did, and above all by the sense He conveyed to them that when they were in His presence they were in the presence of God.

For men who had been brought up on the Old Testament it was inevitable that they should reach the conclusion that this was the long-awaited Messiah. Whatever they meant by this—and many thought more in political terms than in terms of religion—they thought of Messiah as in some sense God's representative on earth, who would rescue Israel from her plight and inaugurate a new and happier era in some way which God would determine. The one thing on which they had never calculated was to see the Messiah on a cross. A crucified Messiah formed no part of Jewish expectation. Accordingly when Passion Week ended unbelievably with the Crucifixion, it is not surprising that in disorder and dismay the followers of Jesus fled for their lives. Their hopes and dreams had become a nightmare.

It is, however, an equally incontrovertible and astounding fact that a few weeks later these same people embarked on the fantastic enterprise of evangelizing the world. The origin of this daunting undertaking is undoubtedly the fact that in their view the catastrophe of Good Friday had been reversed by what they believed had happened on Easter Day. Their claim was that the Messiah was not dead but gloriously alive, that He had proved to be stronger than death and the forces of evil that had sought to destroy Him.

They claimed moreover that they had not only seen Him but spoken to Him, and that many things that had puzzled them during their association with Him in the course of His ministry had at last become plain. His presence with them now, they maintained, was of a deeper and more vital nature than it had ever been when they had companied together in Galilee, but more than that, He had called them and all who were willing to become associated with them in the same allegiance, into a new community based on love and loyalty to Christ as Lord of all. For all who chose to make this break with their past there was the promise of forgiveness and of new life, and the certainty of a new relationship to God and to one another which would change the face of the world. It was their deep sense that a new era had begun that moved these devout Jews to place alongside the holy Sabbath of their ancestors the Lord's Day, the day of the Resurrection. Moreover, right from the beginning they celebrated the death of Jesus not as a memorial to a dead Master but as a eucharist and as communion with a living Lord.

The evidence for the Resurrection-faith is of course woven into the texture of the whole of the New Testament. For the earliest reference to the event itself we have to turn surprisingly enough not to the gospel narratives of Easter Day but to one of St. Paul's letters to the Corinthian church (1 Cor. 15). This was written before any of the gospels, probably in

A.D. 54, about twenty-five years after the Crucifixion. In this letter the apostle refers to the instruction he had received at his conversion to Christianity about A.D. 32, that is roughly three years after the Crucifixion. What he was told then was that Christ rose from the dead and appeared at various times thereafter to many of His followers (vv. 3–7).

The book of Acts, which was written by St. Luke about A.D. 80, also contains early evidence of the Resurrection-faith. St. Luke had every opportunity to gather information about the beginning of the Church through his association with first generation missionaries, and there is some reason to believe that he may have made a preliminary draft of his gospel as early as A.D. 60 or thereabouts. St. Luke was a careful recorder so that when he summarizes the sermons of St. Peter at Pentecost and later (chs. 2, 4, 10) we may take it that this represents the substance of what Christian missionaries in general proclaimed as the essence of the new faith.

The narrative of Acts (ch. 2) indicates that seven weeks after the Crucifixion, on the first Whitsunday, the apostles began their mission in Jerusalem based on the claim that their own belief that Jesus was the long-promised Messiah had been proved by His Resurrection. The heart of the missionary preaching was that God had raised the dead Jesus, whom all their hearers remembered for His 'mighty works', and had exalted Him as Lord. The gift of His Holy Spirit, evidence of which all present could see with their own eyes, was available to everyone who committed himself to Christ in repentance and baptism.

It is clear beyond a shadow of doubt that whether the Resurrection ever happened or not, it was the pivot round which Christian missionary preaching revolved and the unique and startling element in apostolic doctrine. There was no suggestion by the disciples or their followers that Jesus was immortal in the sense that His soul lived on, or merely that His influence was still active among those who had been associated with Him. It was on the contrary a stark claim that between Good Friday and Easter Day the supreme miracle of all time had happened: the dead body of Jesus which had been laid in the tomb had then been raised up and subsequently for the next few weeks until His Ascension Christ had appeared to His followers either as individuals or in groups.

There was a time when miracles were dismissed on the grounds that they violated the laws of nature. Nowadays we are much more cautious. We recognize that the laws of nature are merely what we have been able to establish as the normal way things happen in such fields of study and human experience as we can investigate. We are, however, more and more conscious of the vast amount that we still do not know, particularly in the relationship between mind and body, or, more generally, between what for want of better words we must call the 'spiritual' and the 'material'. A miracle which involves these two factors may not necessarily break the laws of nature, if it takes place in accordance with a higher law or a higher order of being than we yet know.

Obviously we cannot prove the truth of a miracle any more than we can prove the existence of God. In these matters there is no mathematical certainty and it is no more possible to convince someone who is determined to believe that miracles— including the Resurrection—are impossible than it is to persuade an atheist by argument of the existence of God. To anyone with an open mind, however, we can talk in terms of reasonable probability, in the sense that if a number of signposts point in the same direction it is likely that what they point to is in fact there.

Historical Evidence

Historical evidence for the Resurrection is extremely strong. It has been called the best attested fact in history. Frank Morison, who wrote *Who Moved The Stone?*, adducing factual evidence of the truth of the Resurrection, began by undertaking a research project to disprove that it had ever happened, but was forced by his own investigation to come to the opposite conclusion. His method may not be altogether satisfactory but at least he reaches his verdict by a dispassionate examination of the records.

When we turn to the narratives of the Resurrection in the four gospels it is not surprising to find that there are minor discrepancies in their accounts. We are dealing here with oral tradition, current in four different centres of the Church, which eventually was shaped into written records and, as we now have it, conveyed through the differing viewpoints of four separate evangelists. This is bound to lead to some divergence in detail. Further, the incident described was on any showing the most startling event in history. It is difficult enough to get agreement among witnesses in a court of law on much less shattering occurrences such as murders, assaults, plane or train disasters, to say nothing of the discrepancies in any three newspaper accounts of the same football match.

Unanimity among the gospels on all the details of what happened on Easter Day and subsequently would therefore be highly suspicious and would suggest a concocted story. In fact when we examine the narratives the discrepancies are what might be expected—such as the names of the women who found the tomb empty, their reactions when they discovered it, whom they saw at the grave, and whether Jesus appeared to the disciples in Jerusalem or Galilee.

Far more impressive are the points on which the four gospels agree. They have been listed by James Martin in his admirable little book: *Did Jesus Rise From The Dead?* (p. 36).

1. That Jesus was crucified on the Friday of Passover week.
2. That Joseph of Arimathaea successfully petitioned Pilate for permission to bury the body of the dead Jesus.
3. That the dead body was swathed in linen, as the custom was, before burial.
4. That burial was made in a 'rock' tomb (i.e. a cave with a cartwheel stone at the entrance).

73

5. That women followers of Jesus visited His tomb early on the following Sunday.
6. That they found that the stone sealing the grave had been rolled away, and that the body of Jesus had gone.
7. That a message was given them there that Jesus was risen.
8. That the Risen Jesus appeared to His followers (to individuals and to groups) a number of times between that day and Pentecost.

Two main points emerge: firstly, that the tomb was empty and, secondly, that the Risen Christ appeared to His friends. For many people the second point presents less difficulty than the first. They find it easier to think of Christ appearing than of His body disappearing. Yet the one feature of the Resurrection that was apparently common ground between the disciples and their enemies, the Jewish authorities, was that the tomb was empty. St. Matthew's gospel informs us that the Jews alleged that the disciples had stolen the body, not that the tomb was not empty.

Supposing the story of the Resurrection is untrue, what other explanation can there be? Did the women go to the wrong tomb by mistake? If so then the opponents of the first missionaries had only to go to the right tomb to disprove their claim. Or is it perhaps the case that the body of Jesus was stolen by the disciples, or sympathizers, or even by Joseph of Arimathaea himself, who then proceeded to allege that Christ had risen? If this were so it would mean that the founders of the Church were liars and cheats, that the Christian faith was built upon a fraud for which nevertheless its perpetrators were willing to die.

Another possibility might be that it was the enemies of Jesus—the Pharisees or agents of the priests—who stole the body to prevent its subsequent veneration. Surely in that case when the Nazarenes claimed that their Master had risen from the tomb, it would have been simplicity itself to explode their story by producing the body. Or again Jesus may not

74

have been dead when the tomb was closed. If He had only swooned, He may later have managed to crawl out somehow and rejoin His followers. But could such a pitiful half-dead Messiah ever have given rise to a story whose keynote is victory and triumph over death?

The fact is that when seven weeks after the Crucifixion the disciples were proclaiming the Resurrection it was obviously in the interests of the authorities to kill their story. They did not do so because they could not produce the body. Many have found St. John's description of the grave-clothes a strangely convincing element in the narrative—suggesting the linen wrappings round the body lying flat under the weight of the spices, with the head-cloth still in shape, exactly as they had contained the body of Jesus before He left them (John 19. 40; 20. 6–7).

But of course the evidence for the Resurrection is not confined to the empty tomb. This alone would not have been enough to persuade His followers who were in any case not expecting such a thing to happen. What did persuade them that Christ had risen was that on Easter Day He appeared among them and spoke to them. Between then and Ascension Day ten appearances of the Lord are referred to in the New Testament involving various disciples and women followers. In all probability this is merely a selection of many more similar occasions in the same period.

It was through these appearances of the Risen Christ that the disciples came to understand the meaning of the empty tomb. But while many people would not deny that the disciples believed that the Risen Lord had appeared to them, many more find it impossible to agree that He did. No one has ever disputed either that Jesus' followers believed that these encounters had taken place or that they built the Christian faith upon them.

But may it not have been some sort of hallucination? Perhaps they merely saw what they hoped to see. On the contrary, all the evidence goes to show that the Resurrection was the last thing they expected and that at first they were not prepared to believe it. When the women returned from the sepulchre with the news, it was dismissed as idle talk. Even after several appearances of the Risen Christ, St. Thomas was still sceptical, and Doubting Thomas was not alone among the disciples. We are told that many worshipped but some doubted (Matt. 28. 17). We have to ask ourselves whether such people —hard-headed fishermen, a tax-collector, an ex-guerrilla— were the type who have hallucinations, whether they were highly-strung, nervous or hysterical. The women at the sepulchre may have been that but surely not the disciples.

The Risen Christ

Indeed we cannot avoid the impression that the appearances of Christ after the Resurrection were of a singularly unexciting character. There was no mass-suggestion, no mere subjective or even objective visions, but rather a somewhat prosaic series of appearances first to one and then to another, stretching farther and farther away from the sepulchre in a purposeful and clearly designed pattern. We are left with the conclusion that this was a deliberate plan of the Risen Christ to convince His followers beyond any shadow of doubt that He was alive and not dead, that He was no longer tied to any one place, that He was with them still in an even deeper way than during His ministry, so that they could now embark on the mission of the Church preaching a living Lord and not a dead hero.

Quite clearly we must distinguish between the fact of the Resurrection and the manner of the Resurrection. However much evidence is produced which points to the fact that the tomb was empty and that Christ did appear to the disciples, we are left with some problems unanswered. How, for example, was the stone rolled away? Some may be persuaded by Frank Morison's theory that the guards were responsible (cf. *Who Moved The Stone?* ch. 13). More difficult to explain is the nature of Christ's resurrected body, in that it seemed to be the same body but was yet somehow different (cf. John 20. 15; Luke 24. 16). It was recognizable as Jesus, it was tangible but not subject to ordinary laws since it could appear and disappear at will.

What St. Paul has to say about the nature of the resurrection-body in 1 Cor. 15 may help us to penetrate the mystery if not to solve it. He describes the character of the body in the after-life as a 'spiritual' body, that is, not a resuscitation of our present physical bodies or some ghostly disembodied existence but a transformed, changed or 'glorified' body. If we can apply such words as 'spiritual' and 'glorified' to the body of Christ during the post-Resurrection appearances, admitting that they only hint at a truth which we cannot fully understand, we may think of the Transfiguration (Mark 9. 2–8) as a foreshadowing of a kind of body suited to a higher kind of life just as a body of flesh and blood is suited to life in the world that we know. At best, however, anything we can say about life in a dimension which is beyond our present limited experience is speculative and of doubtful value. The real difficulty is for the caterpillar to understand what it is like to be a butterfly.

Talleyrand was once asked how one could found a new religion. His reply was: "Get yourself crucified and rise on the third day." C. E. M. Joad once said that if he were allowed to interview any great personality in past history he would above all want to meet Jesus of Nazareth and ask Him the most important question in the world: "Did you or did you not rise from the dead?" It must be conceded by all but the most sceptical that despite the difficulties involved in understanding *how* the Resurrection took place, the historical evidence that the Resurrection *did* take place is very strong. Unless we maintain that the gospels and epistles are merely a mixture of legend and fantasy, or unless we insist that the Church was founded on a deliberate fraud or by a crazy gang subject to hallucinations and brain-storms, the conclusion is inescapable that a unique event in history happened on the first Easter Day.

77

It has been said that the Resurrection comes dangerously near to proving Christianity to be true. Obviously Christianity cannot be proved true nor can the Resurrection, any more than we can prove that God created the world or that there is a God at all. We are not dealing with cast-iron certainties but with reasonable probabilities, in which case we may think it highly reasonable that the most perfect life of which we have any record should not come to an untimely end on a Cross through malice, ignorance and stupidity. If this were the ultimate truth about human existence it would seem that we live in a singularly pointless universe. We might rather on the other hand think it highly reasonable that Jesus had the kind of life which as St. Peter said could not be kept in death's grip (Acts 2. 24).

Nevertheless such arguments as we have been considering will never convince anyone that Jesus rose from the dead unless he has on other grounds come to some kind of religious conviction and to some kind of encounter with God. This is the weakness of books like: *Who Moved The Stone?* It is right that we should recognize that the Christian doctrine of the Resurrection of Jesus does not rest on fairy tales but on solid intelligible evidence. But it is also right that we should remember that the real significance of the Resurrection only comes home to us when we take the venture of faith and commit our lives to God within the fellowship of the Church.

In the last resort the best proof of the Resurrection, with its implications of victory over frustration, failure, pain and death, is not any recital of historical evidence but the testimony of the countless men and women within the Church for the past two thousand years who have come to know the power of the Risen Christ in their own lives and who have been led through that experience to echo Doubting Thomas's confession: "My Lord and my God" (John 20. 28).

Chapter Seven

THE BIRTH OF JESUS
AND THE HIDDEN YEARS

THE Resurrection convinced the first Christians that the Jesus whom they had come to recognize as the Messiah promised in Old Testament psalms and prophecies must now be thought of as identified in a much more fundamental way with God. How to express this relationship was not so easy. As devout Jews, brought up to believe as the cardinal principle of their faith that the Lord God was one, they could not bring themselves readily to equate Jesus with God. Preferring such titles as the Wisdom of God, or the Word, or above all Son of God, they sought to preserve some kind of distinction. But the distinction was in fact more apparent than real. They prayed to Christ and offered Him worship as in their earlier days they had done to the God of their fathers.

It was not that they substituted belief in Christ for belief in God. Rather was it that as they had come to know Jesus they felt that they had now fully come to know God. In Christ they had encountered God in everyday life in a living person, and now after the Ascension they acknowledged Him as Lord. In so doing they used of Him the word that the Old Testament had used for God, and even despite their Jewish hesitancy to develop the full implications of their faith—which led ultimately to the doctrine of the Trinity—it was as God-man that they thought of Jesus after the Resurrection. By the same token it was as man-God that they now looked back on Him as He had moved among them in Galilee and Jersualem.

We may as well give up any hope of doing more than arriving at an intuitive understanding of what this means. If we are to accept the evidence of the New Testament we are face to face with a paradox which defies rational explanation. We may talk of the two aspects of Jesus' personality—divine and human—or of two natures in one person, of the Word becoming flesh or of God being made man. At best all are attempts to express in words what is ultimately inexpressible, a unique Person who was quite clearly in one sense a man like any other man, but in another sense like no other man who has ever lived.

This is the problem that confronts us in the hazardous enterprise of trying to write a life of Jesus in the twentieth century. But it was no less of a problem for the writers of the gospels. The advance of scientific knowledge, literary and historical criticism of the biblical documents, and deeper insights won for us by anthropologists, psychologists and theologians do not make it basically more difficult for us today than for the writers of the gospels to comprehend the enigma of the person of Christ. Like us they were face to face with a mystery which was ultimately beyond their understanding. Nevertheless they could not possibly refrain from speaking of things that they—or their predecessors—had seen and heard (Acts 4. 20). What they wrote was not so much a biography of the Master but Good News from God for the world and its peoples.

The Virgin Birth

Every gospel—not least that of St. Mark which on the surface is the gospel that brings out most strongly the human characteristics of Jesus—is suffused by this 'mysterious undercurrent'. The very opening words of this earliest record of the ministry of Jesus indicate as much: "The beginning of the gospel of Jesus Christ the Son of God" (Mark 1. 1). Thus the fact that this gospel starts with Jesus' public ministry and says nothing about His birth must not lead us to suppose that if we follow the oldest version of the life of Jesus in the New Testament we can eliminate this awkward problem which is raised in the other three gospels. St. Mark may not specifically try to give some explanation of how the Son of God came to be a carpenter in Nazareth, but he is obviously equally convinced that He did.

The fourth gospel in its prologue (John 1. 1–18) identifies Jesus with the Word, defining this as the agent through whom God created the world. It was, the gospel claims, this medium of the loving purpose of God to bring the whole cosmos not only into being but into a right relationship with Himself, who at a certain point in history became man and was expressed in terms of a human life. Thus for St. John, the point of origin of any life of Jesus is not to be found in Palestine but in the mystery of the Godhead.

The two other gospels, Matthew and Luke, pinpoint Bethlehem as the beginning of their story, but insist that the birth of Jesus was not the result of sexual intercourse between Joseph and Mary, but of the operation of the Holy Spirit upon our Lord's Mother, who became pregnant while still a virgin (Matt. 1. 18–21; Luke 1. 26–38). It is not of the slightest value to adduce evidence in this connection for or against parthenogenesis in the human species or in the animal kingdom. What these gospels maintain is that a unique Person in the history of mankind had a unique beginning—a divine Father and a human Mother.

It is easy enough to dismiss this claim as a re-hash of classical mythology until we remember that the last thing orthodox Jews or Jewish-Christians would do would be to import ideas that were frankly pagan. There must be some other reason, which may simply be that the Virgin Birth of Jesus was a historical fact. Against this it can be argued that it is only specifically mentioned in two out of the four gospels and not at all by St. Paul. It is also the case that Matthew tends to emphasize the miraculous in general and that the first edition of Luke probably did not contain the infancy narratives of the first two chapters.

On the other hand the birth stories in Matthew and Luke are clearly of independent origin, judging by their differences, which points to their early date. It was no part of Old

Testament teaching that Messiah, when he came, should be born of a virgin—indeed virginity was in the Hebrew mind a matter of much less significance than marriage and motherhood. Exaltation of virginity as such was much more a feature of pagan religion, as in the case of the Vestal Virgins. Yet the birth narratives in Luke and Matthew are wholly Jewish and Palestinian in thought and setting.

If the Virgin Birth of Jesus had been invented for doctrinal reasons it is surprising that no further reference is made to it in the New Testament. Indeed it would almost seem as if for Jewish-Christians at any rate it was more important doctrinally to prove Jesus' descent from David, which could only be done by bringing Joseph into the forefront of the picture and to some extent running the risk of contradicting the claim that he was a mere figurehead in the story (Matt. 1. 1–16).

The historical evidence for the Virgin Birth of Jesus is clearly not conclusive. In the nature of the case it is difficult to see how it could be. Certainly since the second century the Church has regarded the Virgin Birth as an essential part of the Christian faith and the creeds in universal use in Christendom affirm it. Further, many will find it more difficult to think of the Jesus of the gospels, unique in power and personality, as the son of a marriage between two obscure Palestinian villagers, however devout the mother or worthy the father, than to feel that a new creative act of God was necessary to produce a new type of manhood.

On the other hand it has to be said that, unlike faith in the fact of the Resurrection, there is no evidence in the New Testament that among early Christians faith in the fact of the Virgin Birth of Jesus was regarded as an indispensable pre-requisite of Christian discipleship. It may also be argued that the insistence of the creeds on our Lord's birth "by the Holy Ghost of the Virgin Mary" was more designed to counter the view that He was not truly human by asserting that He had a human mother, than that He was not the son of a human father. Many modern Christians would go further and say that if

God is to be fully incarnate in the human scene, if Christ is to be fully man, He must be born in the normal way.

If, however, we accept the idea that the Incarnation was a new creative act by which God intended to remake human nature we may well think of the Virgin Birth as the most appropriate means to this end. The two sides of Jesus' personality as evidenced in the gospels would seem to be most adequately accounted for if He had a divine Father and a human Mother. If the Virgin Birth was not integrated into Christian thinking as early as was the Resurrection, it is still unlikely that so ancient a tradition based on the record of Matthew and Luke is part of a mythological framework and not grounded in history.

The Nativity Stories

This is of course not to say that the events surrounding the birth of Jesus as described in Matthew 1–2 and Luke 1–2 are to be treated as a prosaic account of what precisely happened. Theology and poetry, devotion and imagination have given the narratives their present form. But are we therefore to assume that there is nothing of historical substance behind them? The stories of Matthew centre upon Joseph and presumably come originally from him, while the incidents recorded in Luke, focusing attention on the Mother of Jesus, depend ultimately on information which could only be supplied by Mary.

The two accounts do not conflict with one another on major matters, and if we allow for the length of time between the events described and their inclusion in the gospels—at least thirty years longer than the rest of the narratives—as well as the unique nature of the Conception of Jesus, it is not surprising that history becomes interwoven with piety and that they are difficult to disentangle. Some would prefer to think of these birth stories in Matthew and Luke, like the splendid hymns of the Magnificat, the Benedictus, the Nunc Dimittis and the Gloria which they encircle, as wholly devotional in character.

83

They would see the visit of the Wise Men and the Shepherds as symbolic of the homage that has been paid to Christ by learned and simple alike, and the Flight to Egypt as an early token of the Father's providential care for the Son. At the other extreme, the whole sequence of events recorded in these chapters may be dismissed as legend and folk-lore. Historically, it is difficult to identify a universal census at this time (Luke 2. 1) and Josephus, the contemporary Jewish historian, makes no mention of Herod's Massacre of the Innocents (Matt. 2. 16).

On the other hand, there is no real reason why the narratives in Matthew 1–2 and Luke 1–2 should not be substantially historical. Matthew tells of a visit to Palestine by a group of astrologers, presumably from Babylon, the centre of astral observation in the ancient world, who on the appearance of a star of unusual brilliance connected it with the birth of the Messiah whom the Jews had been expecting for centuries. Astronomers reckon that Halley's Comet appeared in 12 B.C., and that a conjunction of Jupiter and Saturn in 7 B.C. would produce the appearance of a single star of striking brightness. When we remember that on other grounds the birth of Jesus is now reckoned to have taken place somewhere between 11 B.C. and 6 B.C., and if we allow time for the journey, there may well be a solid basis in fact behind the Matthew story.

There is also nothing inherently improbable in the story that Herod the Great, a notoriously cruel ruler and in his latter years mentally unbalanced, should have ordered a massacre of infants up to two years old in the town of Bethlehem, the ancient home of David, from whose descendants the Messiah was expected to come and who in Herod's view would be a threat to the throne. Nor is it easy to dismiss the tradition that Joseph and Mary took the child Jesus across the frontier into Egypt for safety. It was a natural refuge so long as the old king was still alive.

The narratives peculiar to Luke 1–2 are concerned with the birth of John the Baptist who is shown from the outset to be the forerunner of Jesus, as well as being a blood-relation. John's parents, Zacharias and Elizabeth, like the elderly Simeon and Anna in the Temple, must have been typical of the pious Jews of the day, whose thoughts were much occupied with the long-expected Messiah. So also, if less dramatically than is related in the gospel, the band of shepherds in the fields near Bethlehem may have had reason to believe that the Messiah had at last arrived in their midst and hastened to visit His birthplace.

If therefore we detach these stories from the atmosphere of fairyland which has come to surround Christmas, and if we recognize that celestial choirs and angelic visitants are part of the stock-in-trade of imaginative popular piety of two thousand years ago, we may come not unreasonably to the conclusion that we have in these early chapters of Matthew and Luke ancient traditions which deserve to be treated as being substantially true.

Nazareth may have been the original home of Joseph and Mary, as St. Luke's gospel has it, or they may have made their home there later, as in Matthew's account. Both gospels agree that the Child was born in Bethlehem and Luke's moving description of the Virgin Mother being driven from the crowded caravanserai to bear her Son in a stable and cradle Him in a manger is surely not merely included for artistic effect or as a parable of our Lord's humility. Astrologers reading the signs in the heavens and shepherds following another type of heavenly sign pay homage to the Child they believe to be the long awaited Messiah.

King Herod, in fear of a rival claimant to the throne, orders the massacre of the infants of Bethlehem and Joseph and Mary flee with the Child for safety to Egypt. After the old king's death they return to Palestine and settle in the town of Nazareth in Galilee where Joseph followed his carpenter's trade (Matt. 13. 55). We are told that the infant Jesus was circumcized according to Jewish practice and dedicated to God in the Temple at Jerusalem (Luke 2. 21–22). Apart from one solitary incident when as a boy of twelve on a visit with His parents to Jerusalem at Passover-time, Jesus was so absorbed in the talk of the learned rabbis that His parents had to come back and fetch Him, we are told nothing at all about what happened for the next thirty years (Luke 2. 41–51).

The Hidden Years

All four gospels begin their detailed account of the life and teaching of Jesus at the point where John the Baptist inaugurates a religious revival which brings Jesus down from Nazareth to the banks of the Jordan near Jericho, the scene of John's mission. At that time, St. Luke tells us (3. 23) Jesus was about thirty years old. This is not as reliable a guide as it seems since John 8. 57 appears to imply that He was in His forties, and no gospel suggests that His public ministry lasted more than three years.

We can, however, say that for at least thirty years between His birth and His association with John the Baptist the life of Jesus is relatively speaking a closed book. These Hidden Years have of course offered plenty of opportunities for conjecture, the most recent being that at some point during this time Jesus was a member of the community of Qumran, the sect which produced the Dead Sea Scrolls. There is no more evidence or likelihood of this than of any similar speculations.

Such indications as the gospels give us suggest nothing other than that Jesus spent the major part of His life in a small town in Palestine working at His trade as a joiner. Joseph is not mentioned during Jesus' active ministry so it is reasonable to conclude that he had died in the meantime and that Jesus took over the responsibility of the chief breadwinner. There were four other sons and an unspecified number of sisters (Mark 6. 3), who must all have been younger than Jesus unless they were children of Joseph by a previous marriage.

Although nothing is said in the gospels about these Hidden Years it is nevertheless possible to glean from the things Jesus talked about in His parables and in His teaching generally the kind of background against which He grew up. Nazareth was then an insignificant and secluded village lying among the hills of Galilee in a countryside of farms and vineyards. The great caravan route from Asia to Africa which lay below on the coastal plain was connected by trunk roads to the major centres of Galilee, adding to the cosmopolitan character of a district which the orthodox Jews referred to contemptuously as "Galilee of the Gentiles" because of its mixed population. Nazareth, however, lived its life apart from all this.

Jesus was clearly at heart a countryman with a countryman's interests. There is the odd reference to synagogues, market places and city streets, but by far the greater number of His allusions is to farming, to shepherding, to trees and animals and flowers. We get vivid word-pictures of large estates with wealthy landlords and hired men, which can hardly have come from any source other than the experiences of these early years. Ploughing, sowing, harvesting; sheep, goats, foxes, wolves, eagles, dogs, hens—the ordinary life of the Galilean countryside seems to be rooted deeply in Jesus' mind.

Then there are the frequent references to domestic scenes which reflect His early home life: the women grinding corn, the house lit by a solitary lamp, the mending of the old clothes. So with the life of the small town streets where the children play, and men stand about the market place. The impression we get is not one of a poverty-stricken society, but rather of a hard-working community. As a carpenter Jesus would make the yokes and wooden ploughs, the household chests and other domestic furnishings that belonged to His craft.

It is possible too, to gather from the later events of Jesus' life, that His education was like that of all Jews, of a higher standard than was common among neighbouring races. He could read, as He did in the synagogue at Nazareth (Luke 4. 16), and write, as He did to cover His embarrassment when the Pharisees dragged the adulteress before him (John 8. 6, 8). His knowledge of the Scriptures was profound; He quoted widely from the Old Testament. He spoke Aramaic as His mother tongue, but He could read Hebrew, the official language of the synagogue, and also probably speak a little Greek, as in His conversations with Pilate and the Syrophoenician woman (Mark 7. 26).

St. Luke's vignette of the boy Jesus in the Temple at the age of twelve exhibiting a more than ordinary grasp of theological questions, even allowing for the earlier age at which oriental children mature, suggests a mind which was even then concerned with serious matters in advance of His years, and a sense of living in intimate dependence on God. This, as we shall see, is the dominating factor in Jesus' self-consciousness, and one which in these Hidden Years must have made Him feel increasingly His difference from His fellow townsmen and from His own family.

If we are to believe the gospel records at all it is difficult to think that the strange power that He exercised over men and nature which they record came as a sudden revelation to Himself. He must surely have been aware in these Hidden Years that He had an ever deepening sense of power within Himself that must be meant by God to be used for some purpose not yet apparent. It was clearly the news of the mission of John the Baptist that compelled Jesus to make the decision to leave Nazareth, perhaps with the idea of putting His own half-formed thoughts to the test.

It is not wise to speculate on what we cannot know with certainty but the Hidden Years cannot have been empty years. In His small town milieu Jesus gained the understanding of men and women, their loves and hates and hopes and fears which His later work reveals. As a craftsman He learned the hard way the disappointments and satisfactions of an everyday job. As a devout Jew He read the Scriptures, attended the synagogue and learned the meaning of prayer.

St. Luke has probably said the last word: "As Jesus grew up he advanced in wisdom and in favour with God and man" (2. 52).

Chapter Eight

THE BAPTISM AND TEMPTATION OF JESUS

The Herald of the New Age

JUST as there is disagreement among scholars about the exact year in which Jesus was born, so there is no unanimity of opinion as to the interpretation of Luke's apparently precise dating for the appearance of John the Baptist (Luke 3. 1). Although one guess is obviously not as good as another in such matters a good case can be made out for dating the birth of Christ as 6 B.C. and the mission of John the Baptist as A.D. 26. Jesus would thus be thirty-two years old at the time, which is more or less borne out by Luke 3. 23.

In or around A.D. 26, then, this strange prophetic figure appeared on the banks of the Jordan in the neighbourhood of Jericho, where the lush tropical vegetation contrasted strongly with the harsh barren mountains of Judaea which towered above it. The Baptist at once attracted attention since the general view was that the age of the prophets was past (Ps. 74. 9; 1 Macc. 9. 27) and would be revived only when the New Age dawned and Messiah came (1 Macc. 4.46; 14.41; Joel 2.28).

John certainly spoke like the Old Testament prophets in their most uncompromising moods, talking the language of Amos and Isaiah with a forthrightness that had not been heard for many a day. He was in fact in almost all respects an Old Testament character. He came from the 'wilderness', the bare scrubland and mountainous country on the fringe of Palestine which had always been associated with Israel's past before she fell a prey to the lures of civilization. It was from such a setting that the voice of prophecy had come most notably in the past to challenge Israel for her defection from the austere standards of her early upbringing, when in the 'wilderness' of Sinai she had pledged herself under Moses to God and His commandments.

The Baptist looked like a veritable Elijah come back to trouble Israel with the same message of denunciation and warning. He wore the same type of coarse camel hair habit and leather girdle (2 Kings 1. 8), his diet of locusts and wild honey was reminiscent of the sparse fare of the ancient keeper of Israel's conscience (1 Kings 17. 6). Like Elijah, and indeed like all the prophets, John's message was basically a call to the people to return from their present godless ways to the faith and practice of their fathers. But his words had an overtone of startling urgency that compelled attention.

At a time when the oppression of their Roman overlords made many Jews responsive to the highly coloured prognostications of those who saw the solution of all their troubles in a dramatic end of the existing order and its replacement by a new Golden Age in which the Jews would lord it over the Gentiles, in particular the Romans, John the Baptist's message appeared to match the hour. He said in effect that the time had come, the Day of Judgment was at hand. True to his character as an Old Testament prophet, however, he quickly dispelled any illusions his hearers might have that this would be Israel's hour of triumph.

On the contrary, as he said, the fact that they were the children of Abraham would not help them, for the Judgment would be based not on racial distinctions but on moral righteousness. If we are to follow Luke's account of his preaching (3. 7–14) the sins which he stressed were the familiar prophetic targets of greed, extortion and violence. So once again the nation was summoned to repentance and urged to turn from its evil ways before it was too late.

There was, however, a striking difference between the message of the Baptist and that of an eighth-century prophet. The preaching of the prophets had always had a note of urgency. When they spoke of God's Judgment and of the Day when it would fall upon Israel it was always with a sense that the situation brooked no delay. The time for repentance was now for the Judgment was at hand. But in John's preaching not only is the great Day on the point of being ushered in but the Messiah is at any moment to be expected.

The belief that a new Golden Age following the Judgment would be inevitably presided over by the Messiah was not the standard teaching of the Old Testament prophets. It was in the period between the Old and the New Testament that the association of the Messiah with the coming new era had become firmly fixed in popular thought, and it was to people who believed that the two things were inseparable that John was speaking. When Messiah appeared the Golden Age, the Kingdom of God, was bound to be close at hand. John's message was of the imminent advent of One so much greater than himself that he was a mere herald of His coming, unfit to do more than unfasten His shoes.

As a token of the repentance which John called for in preparation for the coming Judgment he baptized his converts in the Jordan, saying at the same time that when Messiah came He would baptize them with the Holy Spirit, as Ezekiel had foretold (Ezek. 36. 25–27) but also with fire (Luke 3. 16). Clearly John regarded himself, his mission and his message as simply preparing the way for the great event that was impending. His campaign fell upon responsive ears. Many were stirred by a challenge that had not been heard in Israel for many a day, and conscious of their need of repentance or fearful of the coming Judgment, or both, they confessed their sins and were baptized in the Jordan. Among those who came to John for baptism was Jesus.

The Baptism of Jesus

According to Luke Jesus and John were related (1. 36) but it is unlikely that this had anything to do with Jesus' journey from Nazareth to the Jordan. The ways of the two men would seem to have lain as far apart as their differing temperaments and attitudes—Jesus, the small town carpenter in the pleasant Galilean countryside, John the solitary ascetic in the bare Judaean hills. As we have seen, although we know nothing of the Hidden Years at Nazareth, they must have been a time of intense thought, of study of the Scriptures, and of a growing consciousness on the part of Jesus that He was not like other men.

What that difference was He may have dimly guessed but it is obvious from the gospels that His Baptism was His first great spiritual crisis. This is strongly brought out not only by the account of the event in the gospels but also by the fact that immediately after it He felt Himself compelled to seek the solitude of the nearby hills where the Temptation took place. Baptism and Temptation are clearly part of one overwhelming experience.

It is easy to see how news of a religious revival would induce Jesus to leave His carpenter's bench to sit at the feet of the new prophet. But why did He submit Himself to baptism? Obviously it cannot have been as a token of His repentance and confession of sin, a symbol of the return of a wayward child to the service of the God whose laws He had flouted. The evidence of the gospels is that there never was a time when Jesus was not consistently obedient to the will of God. Thus His Baptism must be seen in the context and spirit of His whole life, as a deliberate identification of Himself with ordinary men in sharing their experiences.

He believed that the Kingdom of God was at hand, and guessed that He might be God's agent to bring it about. The nation was being summoned to repent, to prepare for the New Age. Some were doing so and were being baptized as a sign of their resolve. But many were unmoved by John's appeal and so Jesus responds on their behalf. Thus we may see in the Baptism of Jesus not merely an act of self-consecration or self-dedication but the first overt act by which Jesus showed that He regarded Himself in some sense as representing the whole people. If He really was the Messiah as He had increasingly come to believe, it was His mission to do for men what men were unable or unwilling to do for themselves.

Mark's account of Jesus' baptismal experience is illuminating (1. 9–11). As He comes out of the water He seems to see the heavens opening and the Spirit of God in the traditional form of a dove coming down upon Him, and to hear a voice say: "Thou art my beloved Son, in thee I am well pleased." We shall return to the exact significance of this combination of two Old Testament texts from Psalm 2. 7 and Isaiah 42. 1, but the general import of the experience is clear. In the symbolism of the descent of the Spirit and the divine voice the Bible is saying that at this moment Jesus became convinced beyond shadow of doubt that He was God's Messiah.

It was a heaven-sent confirmation of all that had through these Hidden Years become increasingly evident to Him— this consciousness of strange power, and of unusually deep spiritual experience which had in the end driven Him to leave Nazareth and seek the prophet on the banks of Jordan. This revelation which came to Jesus at His Baptism, which can only have been described by Himself in later conversations with the disciples, marked the start of His ministry. He had received His commission. He was certain now that He was God's anointed messenger, the Messiah, and that He had been given His unique power from God to use in His service.

The Temptation

Jesus' first reaction after this extraordinary experience was to go off by Himself to think things out. The record suggests that it was in no mood of calm reflection but in turmoil of mind. The Spirit drove Him (Mark 1. 12). What did this Messiahship involve? What did the Scriptures say about it? The gospels tell us that for forty days, meaning merely for some time, but recalling the forty days of Moses on Sinai and of Elijah at Horeb, Jesus was alone in the 'wilderness'. Solitude was easy enough to come by in that wild region where the Jordan flows into the Dead Sea. Tradition locates the spot on Jebel Quarantal near Jericho.

93

We can only know anything of what happened there, as in the case of the Baptism, from Jesus' own lips as He must have told it later to the disciples. But this period of inward struggle and tension which is so typically clothed in the imagery of a personal encounter with Satan, the Tempter, is most naturally understood as our Lord's search for the way in which God's cause could best be served and the Messianic task accomplished. One solution after another is rejected until His final decision is the ministry of service which ends on the Cross.

The story of the three temptations as told by Matthew and Luke represents in a picturesque way what were in fact real possibilities. Basically, however, they were the same temptation, to choose the easier and more popular short-cut to success. The first temptation, to turn stones into bread, may be interpreted as Jesus' natural desire to give His people the kind of Messianic kingdom they were expecting. He knew He had the power and He could see the human need and misery around Him. Why should it not be the Messiah's work to inaugurate a new Golden Age such as men longed for, with peace and plenty, health and happiness. But He realizes that this is not enough. "Man does not live by bread alone" (Deut. 8. 3).

The second line of thought, pictured as the temptation to throw Himself down from the pinnacle of the Temple, is again a natural urge to get quick results. How better could He commend Himself to the people and prove He was the Messiah than by adopting the tactics of the wonder-worker, symbolized by this spectacular stunt right in the heart of Jerusalem. Surely then men would listen to Him and God would see to it that no harm came to His Anointed. But again Jesus dismisses this course as unworthy of His vocation. A second quotation from the Old Testament comes to His aid (Deut. 6. 16). He must not abuse His power. He must not put God to the test.

A third way of fulfilling His mission is likewise attractive. This is represented as the devil showing Him all the kingdoms of the world from the top of a high mountain. If the Temptation took place on Jebel Quarantal He would indeed see from its summit a magnificent panorama of the whole valley of the Jordan stretching up towards Galilee, and down to the shimmering waters of the Salt Sea. Clearly this temptation is to found a world-wide Messianic kingdom, as the Scriptures seemed to foretell, with Israel at its centre and the Gentile kingdoms subdued under her feet. Jesus would rule in righteousness as a greater Judas Maccabaeus and the ancient hopes and prayers of the Jews would be fulfilled. Once more, however, it is an idea that suggests itself only to be condemned. This would not be a Messianic kingdom but a secular imperialism based on force and grounded in evil. Again a word from the Scriptures clinches the matter (Deut. 6. 13).

The only way that the Temptation in the Wilderness makes sense is if Jesus knew that He could have chosen any of these ways to fulfil His destiny as the Saviour of the world. We may well feel that the real answer, the way which in the end He chose and followed, was not far from the surface of His mind but that it was borne in upon Him more and more as inevitable as He dismissed one alternative after another as unworthy. When He returned from His solitary wrestling with His problem in the wilderness His mind was made up and His plan of action settled. Yet if we are to follow the hint given by St. Luke He did not leave these temptations behind in the desert. The devil departed from Him only "for a season" (4. 13). There must have been many a time amid the frustrations and discouragements of His ministry when Jesus was similarly tempted.

The Judaean Ministry

The ensuing course of events is not altogether clear. Luke (4. 14) says that immediately after the Temptation Jesus returned to Galilee and began His ministry there. Matthew (4. 12) and Mark (1. 14) suggest that this did not happen till after John the Baptist had been imprisoned, while the Fourth Gospel (1. 35–3. 24) indicates that after His Baptism Jesus remained for some time in Judaea, visiting Jerusalem, and carrying on a movement on similar lines to that of John near the river Jordan.

Possibly the Fourth Gospel is right. Jesus had a profound regard for John the Baptist, describing him in the most generous terms (Luke 7. 28), and if we are to judge by later hints in the gospels Jesus was no stranger to Judaea and Jerusalem. Further, Jesus' first visit to the Temple (John 2. 13 ff.) would account for the beginning of hostility on the part of the official church, while His later sudden calling of the disciples on the shores of the Lake of Galilee would be more understandable if He had attracted them already in Judaea from John's movement to His own (John 1. 35 ff.).

However long the Judaean ministry lasted it came to an end soon after the imprisonment of the Baptist. John's arrest may have been necessary as Josephus, the Jewish historian, says because Herod feared a rebellion, or as Mark says, it may have come about because of the hostility of Herod's sister-in-law Herodias whom the king had unlawfully married, a marriage which the Baptist had denounced (Mark 6. 14 ff.). It may well have been a mixture of both reasons. At all events it was after this that Jesus returned to Galilee, moved from Nazareth to Capernaum on the lakeside (Matt. 4. 13) and there first began the real work of His public ministry.

John the Baptist

Before we leave the point at which Jesus became clear in His own mind that the role of political and military saviour of His people was less than what total obedience to God demanded, a selling of His soul and a compromise with the powers of evil, we ought perhaps to pause for a moment to take a last look at John the Baptist. He had no illusions about his own importance; he was a herald, a "voice crying in the wilderness" (John 1. 23), the 'best man' at the wedding who is happy to give place to the bridegroom (John 3, 29). Yet on any showing he was an impressive and influential figure.

Many years after his death there were to be found in distant Asia Minor disciples of the Baptist who knew little of Jesus but who were devoted followers of this strange ascetic from the wilds of Judaea (Acts 19. 3). His scathing dismissal of the religious leaders of the Jewish community as the "offspring of vipers" (Matt. 3. 7) was of the same stuff as the condemnation by the great spokesmen of God in the Old Testament of the 'false prophets' who brought religion into disrepute by their facile optimism and hollow piety.

Jesus paid him massive tribute as a strong and virile man of God, a prophet and more than a prophet, the greatest of men. He identified him with Elijah, who according to popular expectation would return to prepare the way for the coming of the Messiah as foretold in Malachi 4. 5. Yet whatever we make of the scene described in the Fourth Gospel (1. 29 ff.) where the Baptist indicated Jesus to his own disciples as the 'Lamb of God', it seems much more likely on the more sober evidence of the synoptic gospels that the Baptist was genuinely puzzled by Jesus. He was so unlike anything that even an honest and sincere man of God like John expected as the Messiah—to say nothing of what the orthodox religious leaders would approve of—that he sent messengers from his prison to ask Jesus point blank if He were indeed the Messiah (Luke 7. 19).

It was not only the Pharisees who drew attention to the fact that John and his followers behaved like proper 'holy men', fasting in the best ecclesiastical tradition, while Jesus and His disciples behaved in our Lord's own words more like guests at a wedding (Mark 2. 18–19). In the unfolding of the record of Jesus, so radical and original that He would conform to no recognized pattern of conventional piety, it should not surprise us that orthodoxy rejected Him when even a prophet in the best Old Testament tradition found it hard to believe that such an unlikely candidate could possibly be the One whom seer and psalmist had confidently predicted.

Jesus, however, while giving the Baptist his full meed of honour and esteem, saw him clearly as the last representative of the old order, raking among the dying embers of an out-moded theology. When He said that "among those born of women none is greater than John" He paid fitting tribute to the end product of a majestic line that stretched from Moses through Malachi. But when He added "he who is least in the kingdom of God is greater than he" (Luke 7. 24–28) He indicated that the gospel He came to preach was no mere continuation of the Old Testament faith but a new and revolutionary conception of the relationship between God and man, and of the kind of life that has to be lived in the world that man has been given to live in.

Chapter Nine

THE GALILEAN MINISTRY

WHEN Jesus returned to Galilee from Judaea it was to a land much more thickly populated than it is today. The lake that formed the heart of the tetrarchy is only thirteen miles long and at its widest point eight miles across, yet on its western side it was lined by an almost continuous chain of towns and villages. From Capernaum in the north, which became the centre of Jesus' ministry, through Magdala, the home of Mary Magdalene, to Tiberias, the chief city, trade and commerce, fishing, shipbuilding and textiles kept a large population busy and prosperous. The Galilean orchards were famous and the export of figs, olives, grapes and pomegranates was a considerable asset.

It was to this crowded land which was His home that Jesus came to inaugurate His Messianic mission. What was His message? On the surface it seemed to be the same as that of John the Baptist. According to St. Mark (1. 15) the substance of His preaching was that "the time has come; the kingdom of God is upon you; repent and believe the Gospel." But in fact this implied considerably more than the Baptist had meant. John's campaign had had as its background the traditional picture that was part and parcel of every Jew's outlook whether he was zealot, moderate or quietist. The Kingdom of God was the new Golden Age which was about to dawn, ushered in by a Messiah, an anointed representative of God. It would involve the end of the world as men knew it, a new heaven and a new earth would be created, and there would be a day of vengeance when the unrighteous would be punished. John's message was not good news but bad news for most of his listeners: his emphasis was on the wrath to come and on a Messiah of fire who would burn the ungodly like chaff (Matt. 3. 12). Austerity was his keynote and his own ascetic life with its independence of all worldly attachments was the type that was to be followed by those who wished to be on the right side when the great Day came.

Jesus, on the other hand, as is quite clear from His whole ministry, took a totally different view. He adopted the old terminology—the idea of the Kingdom of God—but He announced it as a present fact and, as He did with every other traditional concept, He gave it a new meaning. Jesus' message was in short that the Kingdom of God, or more properly the Reign or Rule of God on earth had already begun. At this early stage He did not add that He was the Messiah who had brought it into being. He rather let men judge for themselves, and the leading motif of the record of His ministry is the growing recognition by His followers of who He was, culminating in His own proclamation of His real nature and vocation.

In effect Jesus said that this Kingdom of God for which men had been waiting had now arrived; the time had come towards which all the thoughts and prayers of Israel had been directed. Channelled through Jesus Himself, the power of God was now at work in the world in a vital and dynamic new way to transform the lives of men and to bring them into the right relationship with the heavenly Father from whom they had strayed. This was the Gospel, the Good News. It was not the kind of Kingdom of God that many had expected. It was neither a Day of vengeance nor a political triumph for Israel. Nor had God waited, as the religious leaders had always said He would, until the people had repented and turned to righteousness.

He had rather taken the initiative and out of His own love for men and without any merit on their part, He had inaugurated a New Era (Luke 12. 32). Men should still repent, turn their backs upon their past failure, not, as their religious leaders had said, in order to bring about the Kingdom, but in thankfulness for the sheer goodness of God. The whole of Jesus' teaching and healing ministry was built round this conception that the Reign of God on earth had begun. His miracles were a sign that the power of God was at work among men (Luke 11. 20). His parables were illustrations of God's attitude to men and of man's proper attitude to God.

If men were prepared to receive the Kingdom of God as little children (Mark 10. 15), that is if they were prepared to accept the sovereignty of God over their own lives, and become wholly obedient to him with child-like trust, they would find themselves in a realm where evil had no final hold over them and where God's power was available to help them. The Kingdom of God was in their midst if they only had eyes to see it (Luke 17. 21). What the saints of old had yearned for, Jesus' followers could now enjoy (Matt. 13. 17). The least of them was greater than John the Baptist (Matt. 11. 11) because John had not understood that God's Rule was one of love and not of fear.

How the Good News was Received

According to Luke (4. 15) and Matthew (4. 23) Jesus chose the synagogues of Galilee as the first platform for His new message. This was as natural a choice as that of the first Christian missionaries who used the Jewish synagogues throughout the Roman Empire as the obvious starting point for the propagation of the faith. In both cases the new message was not looked upon by its preachers as a radical departure from the religious heritage of the past but rather as a fulfil-ment. Jesus' teaching that the Kingdom of God had begun was regarded by Him as the realization of all the ancient hopes of Israel.

It is in this spirit that He addresses the gathering in the synagogue at Nazareth, in His first recorded sermon (Luke 4. 16–21). He reads to them from Isaiah 61. 1–2, a significant passage in which He identifies Himself with Isaiah's picture of the Messiah who had been invested with the Spirit of God and anointed to be His minister in preaching good news to the poor, in giving sight to the blind, deliverance to those in trouble and in proclaiming that this was the decisive hour appointed by God. It is noteworthy that Jesus omitted the conclusion of the passage, which said that it was also a time of vengeance.

Jesus' message was rather that this was a time for rejoicing, in keeping with which He does not practise the ascetic habits of John the Baptist, and later He speaks of Himself and His followers as a wedding party (Mark 2. 18–19). This word of hope and assurance of God's love which Jesus brought to the harassed and fearful folk of Galilee—a message that promised that if they believed in Him and in what He told them they would find that the 'good time coming' had in fact come—was received with enthusiasm for two very good reasons.

The first was the personal impact which Jesus made upon them. He spoke, as they said, not like the scribes, their normal religious teachers, but as one "having authority" (Mark 1. 22). They felt that this was no second-hand message, no borrowed ideas, but the words of someone whom they could trust implicitly. They knew instinctively that what He said was true. The second reason was that Jesus' words were accompanied by deeds. He did not merely say that a New Order had begun, that the loving power of God was at work in the world in a strikingly new way. He proved it by what He did, by healing the sick, by curing men of madness, by His obvious mastery over evil and disease in all its forms. So, as later in Jerusalem, "the common people heard him gladly" (Mark 12. 37) and "flocked to him from every quarter" (Mark 1. 45).

Preaching and Healing

Right from the beginning of His ministry Jesus began to build up a nucleus of disciples. The Rule of God could not exist in a vacuum. It demanded a community of men—and later also of women (Luke 8. 1–3)—who were committed to the new life of total obedience to the will of God and who were ready to bring others into His service. The first recruits were four fishermen, men who made their living on the Lake of

Galilee. These two pairs of brothers, Simon, later called Peter, and Andrew, James and John, left their work at Jesus' summons to them to become 'fishers of men'.

St. Mark's gospel gives us a sketch of a typical day in the life of Jesus at this stage in His ministry (1. 21-37). The scene is Capernaum on a Sabbath day. Jesus preached in the synagogue, where, as Mark notes, the authoritative manner of His utterance caused general astonishment. Here was no dry-as-dust exposition of the Law, with annotations by learned rabbis, but the direct word of God. In the synagogue at the time was a man whose mind was deranged. The effect of Jesus' preaching on him was to produce an outburst of insane gabbling which stopped when Jesus addressed him directly and the man was cured. Once again the effect on the spectators was the sense that here was someone whose 'authority' extended over men's ailments as well as over their thoughts.

A little domestic scene follows which bears all the signs of being a personal reminiscence of Peter. It would seem that Jesus and His four disciples returned from the synagogue to Peter's house expecting a meal, only to find that Peter's mother-in-law, who appeared to be in charge of the household, was seized with a fever. As soon as Jesus takes her by the hand the fever leaves her, and she is able to carry on with the household chores.

On the same evening, when the Sabbath was officially over, many who were sick in mind or body were brought by their friends to the house where Jesus was and were healed by Him. The counterpart of this exhausting twenty-four hours gives us an insight into how it was possible for Jesus to carry on a ministry which made such demands. We are told that the next morning long before daybreak He went off by Himself to some quiet place, presumably on the hillside above the town, to recover His strength and tranquillity in communion with God.

St. Mark's gospel has always been noted for its abrupt character. Not only does the word 'straightway' recur again and again, giving an air of breathlessness to the narrative, as if Mark were pressed for time or space, but also we can never be certain whether incidents or sayings are recorded in their present order because one happened after the other or because the evangelist had some other purpose in mind. Yet even if we accept the fact that all we can hope to get at this early stage of Jesus' ministry, before we reach the Passion narrative which reads like a continuous whole, is a series of pen pictures or impressions, they are enough to give us a clear idea of the Galilean period in Jesus' ministry.

Glancing through these chapters of the gospel which deal with this stage of our Lord's activity one cannot help but feel that just as St. Mark has given us a typical day in Jesus' life at this time, so he has selected a variety of incidents which shed light on one facet or another of Jesus' approach to human need. Some features of these stories may be obscure and they may be cast in a first-century Jewish framework which is strange to us today, but there is always a timeless element which is relevant in any age.

When an untouchable and no doubt physically loathsome leper approaches Him He does not drive him out of His presence. He lays His hand on him and heals him (Mark 1. 40–45). When the good friends of a paralysed man are so eager to see their helpless comrade cured that they let him down through the roof of a house which is surrounded by a throng of avid listeners to Jesus' preaching, He rewards their concern by healing the cripple. Not only so but He shows by His words that He sees His healing powers as not merely confined to making a man whole in body but whole in mind as well (Mark 2. 1–12).

No Jews were more detested by their countrymen than those who acted as local tax-collectors for the Roman government. They were vilified by the orthodox and bracketed with sinners. Yet Jesus calls one of them to be His disciple, dines in his house with him and his fellow outcasts from society and justifies His action by asserting that His chief concern is with those whose need is greatest (Mark 2. 13–17). He similarly puts human need above religious tradition when He abrogates the sacred rules of sabbath observance when people are hungry or sick (Mark 2. 23–3. 6).

So as men responded to His message of hope and His healing touch the crowds grew and His fame spread. The synagogues and private houses could no longer contain all those who wanted to hear Him or to be cured by Him. A revealing word of St. Mark describes how the hordes of sick folk who came now even from beyond Galilee and Judaea "fell upon him" (Mark 3. 10) in their eagerness to be made well again. So He has recourse to a little boat which He uses off-shore as a kind of floating pulpit from which He speaks to the throng on the lakeside. We may banish from our mind the idyllic scenes depicted on Victorian Sunday School teaching-aids where an orderly crowd of attentive listeners is grouped round the Master as He speaks gracious words from a grassy knoll. Anyone who knows the clamour of an oriental bazaar can imagine rather the noise, the urgency, the smell of diseased bodies and general confusion which must have put an intolerable strain on Jesus at this time.

The number of Jesus' regular followers had grown considerably and it appears that it was out of them that at this stage He selected twelve to be His close associates but also to preach and heal on His behalf. Four of them were the fishermen who had been with Him from the beginning, Peter, James, John and Andrew, still in the forefront, with eight more to make up the twelve, most of whom play minor roles in subsequent events. The number was obviously a deliberate choice on the part of the Messiah to create the nucleus of a new Israel which would carry out the mission that the twelve tribes of old Israel had failed to accomplish (Mark 3. 13–19).

Opposition Begins

Jesus' ministry was, however, not for long universally greeted with acclamation. In His famous parable of the Sower, spoken from His boat to the lakeside crowds, we can detect His recognition of the failure of the majority of His hearers to respond to His appeal. He describes the hardened listeners, to whom the message of God's love is a stale and time-worn theme; the emotional enthusiasts whose faith wilts at the first whiff of adversity; the self-centred materialists who prefer comfort to compassion and self-indulgence to charity (Mark 4. 1–20).

But there was more to it than that. Open disapproval was also making itself felt. His fellow townsmen at Nazareth were scandalized at what they felt to be the presumption of the local joiner, whose family lived among them. How could this man act like the Messiah, claiming to heal men's bodies and minds? Jesus was forced to admit that "a prophet will always be held in honour, except in his home town, and in his own family" (Matt. 13. 53–58).

The failure of His nearest and dearest to understand Him must have been a greater grief. They came down from Nazareth to take Him home. People were saying that He was out of His mind and His family seems to have shared this view. When He says on their arrival: "Who is my mother? Who are my brothers?" it is not an open disavowal of His own kith and kin, but a recognition that for Him now natural ties had to give place to the larger family circle of the Kingdom of God. As He looks round the group He has been talking to He enfolds them all in the new relationship that transcends blood and birth: "Here are my mother and my brothers! Whoever does the will of God is my brother, my sister, my mother" (Mark 3. 20–21, 31–35).

But of course there was the inevitable and more serious opposition of the ecclesiastical authorities. Relations between Jesus and local Pharisees seem on occasion to have been quite friendly. He dines with one of them in his house (Luke 7. 36). But on the whole the accredited religious leaders of society were against Him. It is not difficult to see why, and no doubt their attitude had something to do with the fact that He forsook the synagogues for an open-air pulpit. They could not approve of any man who mixed with the dregs of society, the "publicans and sinners" of Mark 2. 16. Nor did He behave like a proper 'holy man', following the ascetic habits of the Baptist. Instead they described him as "a glutton and a drinker" (Matt. 11. 19).

A more serious objection was the high-handed manner in which He dealt with the sacred ordinances of the Law, refusing to observe the inviolable sanctity of the sabbath (Mark 2. 23–28). Worst of all He claimed to be able to forgive sins, which was the sole prerogative of God (Mark 2. 7). Not only did the local religious leaders of the towns and villages He visited view Him with disfavour, but representatives from the hierarchy in Jerusalem came down to Galilee to spy on Him (Mark 3. 22). King Herod, too, who had no reason to love new prophets, after his experience with John the Baptist whom he had now finally got rid of, made common cause with the Pharisees (Mark 3. 6).

At Caesarea Philippi

Then Jesus suddenly left Galilee (Mark 7. 24). Partly no doubt it was because Herod's intervention introduced the possibility not so much of physical danger to His person, which Jesus never evaded, but of interference with His further plans. But it is equally likely that He left Galilee to escape from His supporters. The general enthusiasm which His Galilean ministry had aroused continued unabated. It is true that many had fallen away when they found that this was not the political movement they had hoped for or when they found that the conditions of following this new teacher proved too hard (Matt. 11. 20–24).

But it seems as if Jesus realized that the acclamations of most of His ordinary followers were based either on His ability to work wonders or on the hope that some dramatic *coup d'état* was impending. A revealing comment in the Fourth Gospel indicates that at this time there was a move to make

Him king against His will (John 6. 15). There was at any rate no real sign of the repentance that He had called for and the Galilean ministry came to an end. It had lasted for perhaps anything up to two years.

There was a third reason for Jesus' departure from Galilee which was of more significance. As we have seen, Jesus had gathered round Him from the beginning of His ministry a mixed band of followers from whom He had selected twelve for special duties of preaching and healing. They had already been sent out on a trial mission on their own (Mark 6. 7–13). Now it seems that in withdrawing from the crowds in Galilee Jesus had in view the further training of the Twelve.

They at least, unlike the throng who constantly clamoured around Him, had understood something of what He meant by the Kingdom of God and the need for a genuine change of heart. And so, accompanied by them, Jesus went out beyond the bounds of Palestine into the country to the north-west of Galilee, the territory of Tyre and Sidon, and to the federation of ten Greek cities known as the Decapolis. Little is told of the details of this journey and Mark's itinerary is difficult to follow. Perhaps not much happened because the primary need of both Jesus and the Twelve was rest and peace.

It was, however, on this journey that what may be called the turning point in Jesus' ministry was reached. It was on a country road near Caesarea Philippi that Jesus asked a question and got an answer that appears to have decided His future plans. He began by asking the Twelve what they thought was the generally held view of His own status. "Who do men say that I am?" Their reply was that some thought He was John the Baptist, or Elijah, or some prophet come back to life.

Jesus then pressed them further. They were the ones who knew Him best, who had been with Him constantly—"And you, who do you say I am?" It was Peter, the first and greatest of the Twelve, who with a sudden flash of insight replied: "You are the Messiah" (Mark 8. 27–29).

Chapter Ten

WHO DO YOU SAY THAT I AM?

THE question that Jesus put to the disciples at Caesarea Philippi: "Who do you say that I am?" is the most searching of all the searching questions that He put in the course of His ministry. It was fundamental both for Him and for the disciples, as we shall see, but it is equally fundamental for us today. Because in the long run what we think of Jesus' teaching and of His miracles depends on what we think of Jesus Himself. If He was merely a great and good man, the supreme Teacher, the noblest of the prophets, the disappointed reformer, the martyred revolutionary or any of the other categories of this type into which many have put Him, we must ask whether His teaching has any more claim to be authoritative than that of Mahomet or Buddha, and whether His recorded miracles were not a combination of legend, distortion of history and a certain gift of faith-healing.

It is not enough to answer this by saying that apparently in the experience of Christian people Jesus is very much more than any of these classifications of Him. They may be accused of subjectivism, wishful thinking or some other psychological complex. Nor is it enough to say that the Church has always taught that Jesus cannot be confined within any human cateegory. The Church may have invented its dogmas or it may have borrowed them from pagan religions. Both these arguments are useful, and indeed essential, but they must be anchored to history. The faith of the Church and the experience of Christian people can be justified only if they can be shown to be grounded in the record of Jesus in the gospels.

We must try to find the answers to such questions as: What impression did Jesus make on those who lived with Him? What impression does He make on us as we read the gospels? What does He say about Himself? As we read the account of the momentous confession of Peter at Caesarea Philippi: "You are the Messiah", it is clear that it was no dogmatic statement of Jesus that led up to it but rather the cumulative effect of all that Jesus had already done and said. Later we shall look at the words that were used to describe Jesus by His contemporaries, but first let us see what it was about Him that led them to call Him more than a prophet.

The Impression Jesus Made

To the Galilean fisherman, or the Roman centurion (Matt. 8. 9) or the twentieth century reader, the outstanding characteristic of Jesus is His authority. It was this that had astonished the crowd who heard His sermon in the synagogue at Capernaum (Mark 1. 22). Here was someone who spoke not like the official expositors of the Scriptures, although in all conscience they laid down the Law with every semblance of infallibility. In Jesus' preaching there was an entirely new note of personal certainty and assurance.

When the prophets in the old days had delivered their most striking utterances they had prefaced them with the words: 'Thus saith the Lord', and they and their hearers knew that this was no ordinary voice of a religious reformer but a message from Yahweh Himself. But when Jesus spoke He said more than: 'Thus saith the Lord', He said: 'I say'. It is perhaps not so easy in English to realize just how much weight is to be put on Jesus' repeated use of the word: 'I'. In the Greek original where the use of the personal pronoun *ego* always indicates emphasis, it is clear that when Jesus says, 'I say', as He so frequently does, for example, in the Sermon on the Mount, He means an italicized 'I'—'I' in contradistinction to everyone else who had spoken before Him.

No one can read the gospels without remarking how Jesus claims again and again to be the culmination of all that had gone before, the fulfilment of prophecy and of the Law. In

His sermon at Nazareth the note He struck was: Today in me the Scriptures have come true (Luke 4. 21). The religion of the Old Testament and the whole history of Israel He considered to have been an unmistakable preparation for His coming. From the call of Abraham, through the changes and mischances of Israel's story, in the heights and depths of their understanding and experience, there were according to Jesus a far-sighted divine plan and an inevitable divine purpose weaving their way through the whole sequence of events and coming to their climax in Himself.

Nor did He hesitate to set His own authority above the most sacred beliefs of His countrymen. God Had indeed spoken through the Law and the Prophets, but Jesus made it plain that He considered that His own words superseded them. "It was said by them of old time . . . but *I* say". This was no matter of opinion, it was a judgment on the faith and practice of the Old Testament. It was indeed an implicit claim to greater authority than was possessed by any human being in past history.

More than that, He demanded from those who were prepared to be His disciples absolute and unwavering confidence and loyalty. "Follow me", He said, and by that He meant no passing attachment but a complete and utter commitment of the whole personality with all its interests, ambitions and private plans. A man had to give up family, home and all that he possessed before he could be called His disciple (Luke 14. 26). Perhaps most startling of all, Jesus claimed to be able to forgive men their sins (Mark 2. 5).

It is surely not too much to say that anyone making assertions of this kind could be only one of two things, either mad or unique. Some people during Jesus' ministry thought He was out of His mind, and His own relatives seem to have felt that this was the explanation of His extraordinary behaviour (Mark 3. 21). The religious leaders of the time inclined to the same view. They felt that He was a dangerous and blasphemous character suffering from self-deception who must be got out of the way.

But those who were closest to Him had every reason to choose the second alternative. These were men who had no axe to grind like the official churchmen, and no public opinion to worry about like Jesus' own relatives. They had lived with Him and knew Him as He was, not only in public but, more important, in private. They had seen the extraordinary cures that He wrought, the effect of His presence upon all who were diseased or mentally deranged, the strange power that He had over men and nature (Mark 4. 41).

Further, no matter how closely they were drawn to Him in loyalty and devotion they seem always to have felt that there was a gulf between them. The most revealing scene in this connection is Mark's description of Jesus and the disciples on the way to Jerusalem after Peter's confession at Caesarea Philippi, where we are shown Jesus striding ahead with His face set towards the city while the disciples follow behind filled with awe (Mark 10. 32). They had the sense of being in the presence of someone from another world.

Messiah

How then did those who had the most intimate contact with Jesus describe Him? We can see both in the Old Testament and particularly in the additional writings which were produced between the two Testaments, the variety of views that were held about the Messiah and the Kingdom. It is not of any great consequence for our purpose to distinguish all the varying shades of thought which surrounded this idea. The common factors were a belief that one day God would intervene in history and establish a reign of justice, mercy and truth. Associated with this there had come to be the figure of a divinely appointed Messiah (the Hebrew word meaning 'anointed', i.e. set apart and consecrated) who would come from the lineage of David and who would restore the glory of David's Golden Age to Israel.

By some this new Golden Age was regarded as a political triumph for Israel involving the downfall of her enemies, for others it would involve judgment on Israel as well, sifting the righteous from the ungodly. Then again there was the growing idea of a supernatural Messiah who would usher in his Kingdom by a cataclysmic advent and reign over a new heaven and a new earth. All these views seem to have been prevalent in the time of Jesus. John the Baptist seems to have been looking for a supernatural Messiah who would come with a judgment of fire and terror (Luke 3. 7–17) and to have been genuinely puzzled to know whether Jesus indeed was the Messiah he had foretold (Luke 7. 19).

But it is rather in the sense of the divinely appointed human descendant of David that Jesus is hailed by His contemporaries. Thus when Bartimaeus, the blind beggar at the roadside near Jericho, asks Jesus to help him he calls Him "Son of David" (Mark 10. 48), and when the madman in the synagogue at Capernaum calls Him "Holy One of God" (Mark 1. 24) they both mean the same thing—Messiah. Similarly with the titles 'Christ', which is the Greek translation of Messiah (= Anointed), and "Son of God" as it is used by Peter at Caesarea Philippi (Matt. 16. 16) or by the Sanhedrin (Luke 22. 70), the meaning is likewise the official title of Messiah.

In the Old Testament the whole nation had been called God's Son (Exod. 4. 22; Hos. 11. 1; Jer. 31. 9) and in the Psalms the title had been given to the Messianic king (Ps. 2. 7; 89. 27). When Nathanael (John 1. 49) calls Jesus Son of God, he calls Him King of Israel in the same breath, the two terms apparently meaning the same thing. (On the other hand, when the centurion at the Crucifixion says: "Truly this was a Son of God" (Matt. 27. 54) he probably meant no more than Luke's version of the same incident where the centurion says: "Certainly this was a righteous man" (Luke 23. 47) .)

Summing up, then, we may say that apart from the ordinary titles of address such as Rabbi and Master, the impression made by Jesus on those closest to Him was that He was the long-awaited Messiah. To appreciate what that means we should turn to such Old Testament passages as the Messianic prophecies of Isaiah e.g. 11. 1–10 or to some of the Messianic psalms e.g. Ps. 72. For the Jews there was no higher human category than the Messiah. He was to be greater than any of the patriarchs or prophets, greater than Moses or David. He was to be so far above ordinary mortals and so closely connected with God that indeed no human category could properly contain him.

So when Jesus was called Messiah by His contemporaries it meant that in their language, in their thought-forms, they were trying to say that they had in their midst a Person whom they knew to be the carpenter of Nazareth, but who was like no other Person they had ever known or heard of. That He was a man among men there could be no doubt, but His acts and words and manner could only be explained by the belief that God was in Him and working through Him in hitherto unheard of ways which they could only dimly grasp.

This verdict of His contemporaries, that He was the Messiah of God, in so far as it was given in casual encounters with people whom He had healed, or by mentally deranged persons who can sometimes light upon the truth quicker than normally balanced people, was not valued overmuch by Jesus. Much of it was obviously the credulity of impressionable peasants who saw miraculous cures and were prepared to believe at once that the Messianic Age had dawned.

Simon Peter's confession at Caesarea Philippi was, however, a different matter. It not only marked the turning point of Jesus' ministry but it was received by Him as the most important thing ever said to Him. It would seem that what Jesus valued in Peter's avowal was that here was no hasty verdict based on an emotional reaction, but the words of a man who knew Jesus as no one else did, who had lived with Him, seen every side of Him, and who on the basis of that thoroughgoing intimacy acknowledged Him as the Christ.

As we read the solemn words with which Jesus accepted the verdict of Peter: "Blessed art thou, Simon . . . for flesh and blood hath not revealed it unto thee but my Father which

is in heaven" (Matt. 16. 17) we cannot but feel that whatever
Peter or any of his contemporaries felt about Him, Jesus
Himself had never had any doubt of the uniqueness of His
role. Let us therefore turn to the question of what Jesus thought
and said about Himself.

The Sonship of Jesus

It is most revealing to notice how Jesus describes Himself.
In the synoptic gospels He does not ever call Himself Son of
God, Son of David or Messiah, in so many words. Yet throughout the whole narrative it is evident that He was conscious of
a relationship with God that went deeper than any formal
titles. As a boy of twelve in the Temple, as St. Luke tells us
(2. 41–51), He struck the note which was to dominate His
career: He must be in His Father's house. Throughout the
gospels there is not the slightest doubt that Jesus conceived of
Himself as being in a relationship to God which no one else
shared.

When He called God Father He was saying nothing radically
new. Both in the Old Testament and in pagan religions the
idea of the Creator as Father of all created things was already
implicit. But when Jesus called God: "My Father", He was
saying something vastly different. He never allows that distinction to be slurred over. God is: The Father, My Father, or
Your Father, but not except when He is teaching the disciples
how to pray: Our Father.

Now it is quite clear to anyone reading the Fourth Gospel
that Jesus assumes and teaches His unique Sonship to God
throughout. In that gospel where the words "Son of God" are
used they are not used in the same sense as in the synoptic
gospels meaning "a righteous man" or "Messiah". For this
reason those who are determined to reduce Jesus to purely
human categories have been at pains to point out that the
Fourth Gospel, being later in date and consisting so largely of
interpretation rather than 'facts', is not to be trusted in this
matter.

Let us therefore not rely on the Fourth Gospel but let us take three examples from the older sources in the synoptic gospels: two from Mark and one from Q. The Q saying (Matt. 11. 25–27; Luke 10. 21–22) which comes from Jesus' Great Thanksgiving reads as follows: "All things have been delivered unto me of my Father: and no one knoweth the Son, save the Father; neither doth any know the Father, save the Son, and he to whomsoever the Son willeth to reveal him." If this saying had come from St. John it could not have been more Johannine in tone.

The second example is the parable of the Wicked Husbandmen in Mark 12. 1–9. No one reading this can have any doubt as to what Jesus means. God is the owner of the vineyard, the vineyard is Israel, the wicked husbandmen are the Jews. The servants whom the owner sent to collect his revenues are the prophets. They are beaten or killed. At last, says Jesus, the owner of the vineyard sent one whom he thought the tenants would respect, his own dear son. The priests who heard the parable at all events had no doubt as to what Jesus meant (Mark 12. 12).

The third saying comes from Mark 13.32, where Jesus, talking of the Last Days, says that no one knows just when the end will come, not the angels in heaven, nor the Son, but only the Father. These three examples are enough to indicate that if we are to believe anything in the gospels at all, we must believe that Jesus Himself, and not the early Church, spoke of His unique Sonship, stressing on the one side His own unique relationship to God, and pointing on the other to Himself as the only way by which men might reach a true knowledge of God. This sense of Sonship to God was primary with Jesus. It was the foundation of His thinking, His teaching and His actions. It is from this foundation that there arise the other aspects under which Jesus regarded His mission.

Jesus the Servant

When we turn now to the question of how Jesus, conscious

of this peculiarly intimate relation with God, regarded His vocation, we are faced with the curious paradox that though He welcomed Peter's realization that He was the Messiah, it was a title that generally speaking He avoided and discouraged people from using about Him (Mark 3. 12 etc.). The reason was that Jesus had from the beginning been conscious of a quite unprecedented relationship with God. He did in fact regard Himself as in a real sense the fulfilment of Old Testament expectations and prophecies. He believed He was God's Anointed. He was conscious of living from day to day in the presence of God, of being endowed with divine power, and in the great spiritual crises of His life—His Baptism, His Transfiguration and His Agony in Gethsemane—the realization of His isolation from the rest of mankind seems to have been overwhelming.

But it was equally clear to Him that when the men of His time said: 'Messiah', they meant something entirely different from what He meant. To them the Messiah was either a miracle worker, or a political aspirant who would overthrow the Roman oppressors. The Kingdom was for them largely the rule of Israel by courtesy of God, not the rule of God to which Israel like every nation must be subject.

Jesus on the other hand, although he did not openly profess to be the Messiah, tacitly acknowledged that He regarded Himself as indeed the One towards whom men's hopes and prayers for centuries had been turned. This explains His message to John the Baptist, who had sent to ask Him if he were the Messiah: "Go and tell John what you have seen and heard: how the blind recover their sight, the lame walk, the lepers are clean, the deaf hear, the dead are raised to life, the poor are hearing the good news" (Luke 7. 22). John must draw his own conclusions. So must the people who saw Him enter Jerusalem in the manner predicted of the Messiah by the prophet Zechariah (Mark 11. 1 ff.) and so must the High Priest, to whom for the first time Jesus at His trial acknowledged the title as His own (Mark 14. 62).

Jesus, however, gave the ordinary conception of the Messiah, whether that of the Old Testament or of His contemporaries, an entirely new and original orientation. This is the real significance of the words of Scripture that came to Jesus at His Baptism as embodying His divine commission. In that experience Jesus described His self-consecration in two quotations from the Old Testament (Mark 1. 9–11). The first was: "Thou art my beloved Son", which comes from Ps. 2. 7 and is a description of the future King-Messiah. Jesus thus regards Himself as the realization of this hope.

The second quotation: "in whom I am well pleased" is from Isa. 42. 1 and comes from a passage which deals not with the King-Messiah but with the Servant of God who through his own suffering saves his people. This combination of these two quotations and the ideas behind them is highly important because it gives the clue to Jesus' interpretation of His own role and destiny in accordance with which He plans His whole ministry.

He is the Messiah, but His Messiahship is not one of sovereignty over the Gentiles, or indeed over anyone. It is the sovereignty of self-giving, of perfect obedience to God and love to man. No one before Christ had thought of a Messiah who would achieve His ends through suffering. This combination of these two Old Testament concepts— Messiah and Servant—also provides the clue to the nature of the Kingdom. Again it is not a Kingdom of power and might, or merely a vague Rule of God over the hearts and minds of men.

Jesus regards Himself as the Founder and Prototype of a New Order of men and women, the people of the Kingdom. He is Himself the incarnation of the Kingdom, He expresses all that the Reign of God means in human terms. To follow Him is to enter the Kingdom. To take His yoke upon one is more than to learn from Him the lessons of service and obedience which His whole life expresses. It is to become part of the community of which He is the Head.

This leads us to the other aspect of Jesus' sense of vocation which is expressed in the name by which He most frequently describes Himself, the "Son of Man". Sometimes He uses this phrase with no particular meaning beyond an equivalent of the word 'I', as when He says that the Son of Man has nowhere to lay His head (Luke 9. 58). But there is a deeper meaning in the words which once again can be explained only by reference to the Old Testament. If we rule out such uses as in Ps. 144. 3, where it is simply a paraphrase for 'man', or Ezekiel's use of it as a name for himself (Ezek. 2. 1 etc.), the origin of this obscure phrase must be sought in the vision of Daniel 7, where a figure "like unto a son of man" appears and is invested as ruler of the "kingdom of the saints of the Most High."

Although it seems from this vision of Daniel that by the "Son of Man" is meant a human being as opposed to the monsters who ruled the "kingdoms of the world", he has even here a supernatural significance and in intertestamental times the Son of Man came to be identified with the Messiah who would come in judgment in the last days. So when Jesus chooses this relatively unfamiliar name for Himself in preference to the misleading title of Messiah, He is clearly thinking of Himself as one who is destined to future glory and exaltation, who will be invested with an everlasting Kingdom and who will be the Judge of all men. But the prelude to the glory and exaltation must be the way of Isaiah's Servant, the way of suffering, sacrifice and death.

Chapter Eleven

THE MIRACLES

IF the gospels present us with anything like a true picture of the kind of things that were said and done in Palestine during the lifetime of Jesus we have to take into account the fact that not only did Jesus teach a new design for living but He also exercised a new power over disease and death. The earliest record of the preaching of the Christian missionaries, as for example in Acts 2. 22; 10. 38, indicates that one of the foundations on which the claims made for Jesus by the disciples rested was that He was able to perform what we now call miracles—healing the sick, making the lame walk, curing insanity, restoring sight, bringing the dead to life, and other things equally extraordinary.

Whether we like it or not, whether we should prefer that the gospels recorded only His parables and sayings, we cannot escape their unanimous witness that the ministry of Jesus is shot through with a series of remarkable actions in which He displayed a unique power over the human body and the natural world. Any attempt therefore to rule the miraculous element out of the gospels is doomed to failure.

St. Mark, the earliest of them and by general consent the safest guide to what actually happened, is as essentially a gospel of miracles as any of the others. Even in the Q stratum of sayings, earlier than Mark, the miraculous character of Jesus' ministry is implied (Luke 11. 20, Matt. 12. 28; Luke 7. 22, Matt. 11. 4–5). It is thus neither legitimate nor possible to construct any life of Jesus without recognizing that the element of miracle plays a dominant part. We cannot attribute the miraculous either to the inventiveness of the early missionaries or to later legends. From the very beginning these "mighty works" that Jesus did were part of the Good News. We must take the gospels as a whole.

Nor can we eliminate the miracles by explaining them away, because then they would cease to be miracles and there would have been no point in the early missionaries preaching about them or the evangelists recording them. These acts of Jesus and events in His life found their way into the gospels just because they were extraordinary, because they brought men up against a new kind of power and a new order of life. If the dead who were raised up were not really dead but only asleep (e.g. Mark 5. 39), if blind men who received their sight merely appeared to be blind (e.g. Mark 10. 52), and madmen simply affected to be demented (e.g. Mark 5. 1 ff.), the incidents would not have seemed to be sufficiently unusual to the people who saw them to make any impression on them and hence would never have been recorded.

Casting Out Devils

We must of course distinguish between the fact and the framework. Bultmann is right in his claim that we must demythologize the gospels in so far as the setting of the miracles is Palestine in the first century A.D. when the popular conception of the cause of illness was demon-possession. It does not invalidate Bultmann's argument to say that among primitive tribes today the fear of demons is still very real and that by exorcism or what are believed to be magic potions a sick man may be made well, and by imposing a curse on a healthy man who believes in evil spirits the man may die.

Medical science today would not attribute paralysis, deafness, blindness and madness to the action upon the patient of evil spirits. This was however the belief of the writers of the gospels, the victims of the diseases, and the spectators who saw them cured by Jesus. In earlier Old Testament times the good and evil things that happened to men were attributed to God alone. It was His will that a man should either prosper and die in peace or live in misery and die of an incurable illness. As time went on the concept developed of an independent power of evil in the world, which under the influence of Persian dualism, through life under Persian rule for two centuries, crystallized in the period between the Old Testament and the New into a hard and fast doctrine.

God reigned in heaven, above the sky, but Satan, His adversary, ruled on earth. Through His angels and archangels God supervised the natural order and the affairs of men. It was they who distributed mercy and healing, acted as God's messengers to men, carried men's prayers to God, guarded the righteous, and kept a record of good and bad deeds. With God and His angels, Satan and his demons were in constant conflict. These fallen angels were held to be responsible for all temptation, suffering, disease and death. They could possess men's bodies making them mad, they could enter the natural order, causing havoc and disaster.

For a world in the grip of this evil power, which was as much evidenced by Roman oppression as by disease of mind or body, the people of Jesus' day saw no hope short of the advent of the Messiah. When the great day dawned and the Rule of God came upon earth, Satan and his minions would be overpowered and sent to everlasting punishment. What Jesus proclaimed was that this had now begun to happen. Satan was being defeated by the stronger power of God, working through His Messiah. By the healing of men's minds and bodies, and by the breaking of the power of death, the demons were being vanquished and God's will was shown to be done on earth as it was in heaven.

There is no evidence in the gospels that Jesus was accommodating Himself to the popular mythology of His day when He spoke of "casting out Satan", or when He exorcized the evil spirits that possessed the insane. It is as unrealistic to divorce Jesus from the thought-forms which He shared with His contemporaries in this respect as to expect Him to know of the existence of the United States or atomic energy. The Incarnation was a true incarnation. Jesus' factual knowledge was that of a first century Jew. It was His knowledge of values, of the purpose of life, of the mind of God that led men to recognize Him as divine.

It is surely as irrelevant that Jesus believed in demon-possession as that He no doubt believed that the earth was flat. What the gospels record is that His cures were real cures, that through their encounter with Jesus blind men were able to see, lame men were able to walk again, lunatics became sane and dead men lived. The same results would have occurred if Jesus had come at some point in history when demon-possession was not the current explanation of the cause of disease.

When we turn to those miracles of a different kind which are only recorded as having happened once, we cannot rule out the possibility that they may be capable of some simple explanation and that through misunderstanding or the lapse of time they may have taken on a miraculous colour. The story of Jesus' cursing of the fig tree which immediately withered (Matt. 21. 19), for example, may have grown out of a parable spoken by Jesus about an unprofitable tree that bore no fruit, like that in Luke 13. 6–9 where His words clearly refer to Israel's failure to be the people of God. Or a story of this kind could have grown around a particular withered tree, rather like the pillar of rock-salt which presumably gave rise to the story of Lot's wife (Gen. 19. 26).

The so-called "nature miracles" (i.e. Jesus walking on the water, stilling the storm, feeding the multitudes, changing water into wine) may conceivably have had their origin in some ordinary happening which in time became transformed into an extraordinary event. As we know only too well legends of all sorts tend to gather around the personality of any outstanding religious figure, Christian or non-Christian, a St. Francis or a Buddha. We can never be certain that any particular incident happened exactly as it is recorded in the gospels and we must always allow for the human element, the fallibility of observers and the natural tendency to exaggerate.

By the nature of the case, a saying which was presumably often repeated is more likely to be accurately reproduced than an incident once observed. But when all is said and done, allowing for the possibility of misunderstanding or the growth of legendary elements in some particular instances, we are face to face in the gospels with a large number of incidents which defy explanation by ordinary standards. What is to be our attitude towards them?

Three Possible Attitudes to the Miracles

We may of course simply reject them all on the grounds that in our experience and by the laws of nature miracles just do not happen. This could have been said with much more confidence a century ago than it can be said today. At that time it appeared not only that the universe moved in fixed unalterable grooves but that it was governed by inflexible laws, all of which had been discovered. Now, however, we are surrounded by things which a hundred years ago would have been regarded as miraculous, in medical science, television, space-travel, and automation.

In this atomic age we are much less certain that we understand the laws of nature and that there is no room for the incalculable and the unexpected. We are in a much less dogmatic frame of mind about what can and what cannot happen, and much more inclined to think that we are only beginning to understand a fraction of the hidden mysteries of the universe. Have we fully explored the relationship between mind and matter? Is the material world set over against a spiritual world which cannot influence or affect it? Is it impossible that there may be higher laws of nature than those known to us in accordance with which surprising things may happen? If we cannot confidently answer: Yes! to questions like these we are not entitled to approach the question of miracles with a closed mind.

Another possible attitude towards the miraculous element in the life of Jesus is to say that we can believe in some of His miracles but not in others. The difficulty of this point of view is one of discrimination. If it is to be a question of which miracles are true and which are untrue, who is to be the final arbiter? How can we guard against personal predilections and prejudices? On what grounds should we reject one miracle and accept another?

Is a miracle to be believed if it occurs in Mark but not if it appears in John? Are we to accept the healing miracles and reject the "nature miracles", or must we distinguish between 'probable' healing miracles like the curing of a mental derangement and 'improbable' ones like the raising of Lazarus? Or again, is our criterion to be that we accept only those miracles which bear some resemblance to the possibilities of twentieth century medicine? Clearly this eclectic method is much too difficult and arbitrary to be reliable.

The third possibility is to accept the miracles which appear in the gospels as a record of what actually happened, a record not necessarily accurate in every detail and subject to fallible human reporters but substantially true. This would seem to be the most reasonable view in that it gives the gospels credit for being genuine and not fraudulent; it recognizes that in the person of Jesus we are in contact with someone who was in every way unique and who may therefore be expected to have a unique effect upon men and upon His environment; and it admits that there are some things which science cannot yet explain about the interaction of the physical and the spiritual.

The Record of the Miracles[1]

With these considerations in mind let us look at the gospel records. Perhaps the first point worth noting is that miracles were not credited to all and sundry. In other words we cannot account for the miraculous element in the gospels by saying that they were written in a superstitious and credulous age in which wonder-working and supernatural powers were attributed to any great religious leader. On the contrary it is

[1]Here I follow Edwin Lewis's classification of the gospel miracles.

expressly stated that John the Baptist, unlike Jesus, performed no miracles (John 10. 41). The hocus-pocus of the pagan magicians whom the first missionaries encountered (Acts 8. 9; 13. 8) had no counterpart in Jewish society. Clearly the 'mighty works' of the gospels are regarded as the result of some peculiar power connected with Jesus, able to be communicated by Him (Mark 6. 7), but bound up with the coming of the Messiah and the New Order.

A second point to be considered is that apparently only a fraction of the miracles that Jesus performed have been recorded. About thirty-five of them are described in the gospels, some of them at length (e.g. the curing of the Gadarene madman (Mark 5. 1–13), the raising of Jairus' daughter (Mark 5. 22–24; 35–43), the feeding of the five thousand (Mark 6. 32–44), the changing of water into wine (John 2. 1–11), the healing of the paralysed man (John 5. 1–18), the cure of the blind man (John 9. 1–41) and the raising of Lazarus (John 11. 17–44)). Other miracles are little more than mentioned, (e.g. the healing of Peter's mother-in-law (Mark 1. 29–31) or of the dumb man (Matt. 9. 32–33)).

But in addition to these localized and specific incidents there are several comprehensive statements in the gospels which indicate that Jesus performed far more cures than would appear from the records. Sentences like the following from Matt. 9. 35 crop up repeatedly: "Jesus went about all the cities and the villages, teaching in their synagogues and preaching the gospel of the kingdom, and healing all manner of disease and all manner of sickness" (e.g. Mark 1. 32-34; 3. 10; 6. 55-56; Luke 6. 17–18; 7. 21; 9. 11; John 6. 2; 20. 30).

It is obvious therefore that only a sprinkling of the total number of cures has found its way into the gospels. Instead of there being any likelihood of exaggeration in the record, it suffers much more from understatement. St. John is perhaps thinking of this when he says that "the world itself would not contain the books" that might have been written about the ministry of Jesus (21. 25).

The third impression we get from the gospels is that what we are given there is a selection of typical cures. From among all the cases of mental disturbance which Mark mentions in 1. 32 as having been healed on a certain sabbath day in Capernaum, he selects one for detailed description (1. 23–27). Similarly in 7. 31–35 he gives a sample of Jesus curing a deaf-stammerer out of all the miracles that took place after Jesus came back from Tyre and Sidon (Matt. 15. 29–31). So we are given a typical case of people being cured simply by a touch of Jesus or by touching Him unawares (Mark 5. 25–34; 6. 56). Blindness is often mentioned as one of the commonest afflictions which Jesus healed but the gospels give us only a few instances (e.g. Mark 8. 22–26; 10. 46–52; John 9. 1–41).

Distinct from the miracles of healing which seem to have been innumerable, there were certain miracles of a different character which appear to have happened only once or at the most twice or thrice. It is for example only once recorded that Jesus walked on the Lake of Galilee (Mark 6. 45–52), or stilled a tempest there (Mark 4. 35–41); twice He is said to have fed a vast crowd with practically no provisions (Mark 6. 30-44; 8. 1-9); three times He is credited with having raised the dead (Jairus' daughter in Mark 5. 22–24, 35–43; the son of the widow of Nain—Luke 7. 11–16; and Lazarus—John 11).

It is at this point that the minds of many people who are prepared to allow that Jesus was able to perform cures of all descriptions stop short at conceding that miracles of this latter type can be at all historical. They seem to them to come into the realm of black magic. Can this honest doubt be met? First of all, let us not make the problem more difficult than it need be. Certain incidents of this kind which are sometimes regarded as miraculous are not necessarily miraculous at all.

The blasting of the fig tree may, as we have seen, be an embellishment of an acted parable (Matt. 21. 18–22 compared with Luke 13. 6–9). The great draughts of fishes (Luke 5. 4–10; John 21. 4–11) may well be allegories of the mission of the Church as fishers of men under the guidance of Christ,

127

and the story of the coin in the fish's mouth (Matt. 17. 24–27) may have originated in a jesting remark of Jesus to Peter. The coin is not in fact said to have been produced. In the case of the water being changed into wine (John 2. 1–10) it is plainly not being suggested that our Lord miraculously provided an additional hundred and twenty gallons of wine at a wedding when the guests had already had enough to drink. It is surely a parable of the replacement of the thin water of Judaism by the rich wine of the Gospel. The alleged transference by Jesus of the 'unclean spirits' which possessed the Gadarene demoniac into a herd of swine which thereupon rushed headlong into the Lake of Galilee is much more likely to have originated in the animals panicking at the paroxysms of the maniac as he was cured (Mark 5. 1–13).

Some will prefer to rationalize the story of Jesus walking on the water by saying that He was probably walking *in* the water near the shore; or that He stilled the storm because it subsided from natural causes as often happens suddenly on the Lake of Galilee; or that the multitudes were fed because Jesus' example of sharing communicated itself to those who had brought their own provisions but had intended to keep them for themselves.

Explanations of this kind would certainly not have satisfied the evangelists. In their minds such incidents were demonstrations of the power of the Messiah. The winds and waves obeyed Him as the psalmist had said they obeyed the command of God (Ps. 107. 23–30). The sharing out of the loaves and fishes, first to the Jews (Mark 6) then to the Gentiles (Mark 8), were foreshadowings of the Messianic banquet in the Kingdom of God (Luke 14. 16–24), sacramental occasions on which the Messiah fed His people with the Bread of Life.

The question as to whether Jesus *could* have walked on the water, stilled the storm or fed the multitude with a few loaves and fishes can only be answered in the light of our view of who Jesus was. If we believe He was God made man, voluntarily taking the flesh and blood of ordinary humanity for man's redemption, we cannot dismiss these actions as impossible for

Him. They will be seen as moments when the divine power is manifested, operating in accordance with a higher law than we know, even through a true incarnation.

Our view of the Person of Christ would also condition our attitude to those instances where He is said to have raised the dead. It is sometimes suggested that Jairus' daughter was in fact only asleep as Jesus is quoted as having said (Mark 5. 39) and that the story of Lazarus (John 11) is merely told by the Fourth Evangelist as a peg on which to hang his teaching about death, life and resurrection. The restoration to life of the son of the widow of Nain, however (Luke 7. 11–16), does not seem to be capable of any rationalization, and if one such miracle is accepted there seems to be no good reason why the others should not be treated likewise. Although all three who were brought back from death must have died later in the normal course of events, it is striking that these are all cases of peculiar poignancy; a small child, the son of a widow, and a personal friend. Jesus may well have felt that they called for the exercise of a power which He seldom used.

The argument that the healing miracles (except the raising of the dead to life) may be accepted, while the nature miracles must in some fashion be explained away as misunderstandings or pious tales, is based upon an alleged difference in technique. It is said, for example, that the healing miracles are borne out by modern medical and psychiatric practice, and that they are bound up with the patients' co-operation in the act of healing, in other words that the healing miracles are in fact faith-cures. Let us therefore examine Jesus' healing methods in the miracles that are recorded.

Jesus' Healing Methods

Jesus had apparently no fixed method of performing His cures, or at least no stereotyped procedure is recorded in the gospels, although allowance must be made for the fact that the evangelists do not always describe an incident in exactly the same way. In the story of Jesus' Arrest in the Garden of

Gethsemane, for example, all four gospels record that one of Jesus' supporters (identified as St. Peter in the Fourth Gospel— 18. 10) attacked the servant of the High Priest and severed his ear. Only St. Luke, however, adds that Jesus healed the man, and in this case He does it with a touch (22. 51).

Other cases where merely to touch Jesus is sufficient to effect a cure are that of the woman with a haemorrhage who touched the hem of His garment while the crowd thronged around Him (Mark 5. 25–34) and the unspecified cures referred to in Mark 6. 56 and Luke 6. 19. There are, however, other cases again where Jesus not only touches the sufferer but speaks to the patient as well. This happens in Luke's version of the story of the cure of St. Peter's mother-in-law from a fever (4. 39), at the restoration to life of the little daughter of Jairus (Mark 5. 41), at the cures of a leper (Mark 1. 41), of two blind men (Matt. 9. 27–31) and of a woman who was crippled with arthritis (Luke 13. 10–13).

There are on the other hand some instances where Jesus does indeed seem to invite the co-operation of the sufferer. This may be achieved by a heightening of the tension in the patient's mind before the cure, as in the story of the healing of Bartimaeus, the blind beggar of Jericho (Mark 10. 46–52) and of the paralysed man at the pool of Bethesda (John 5. 2–9). Or Jesus may perform certain actions which seem designed to awaken confidence in the patient, as in the rather elaborate technique of Mark 7. 33–35; 8. 22–25; John 9. 6. Again He exorcizes the demons who were believed to cause epilepsy and mental disorders, thus doubtless encouraging the belief of the person possessed in His power to cure him (Mark 9. 14–27; 5. 1–15).

From an examination of the evidence therefore it does not appear that we are entitled to make any clear-cut distinction between the nature miracles and the healing miracles, for the healing miracles were not invariably performed through the co-operation of the sufferer. It may be said of course that the very fact that people came at all to Jesus to be touched, or that they were brought by their relatives, indicates faith on the part of the patient or his friends that Jesus could heal them. St. Mark expressly says that Jesus was unable to exercise His healing power to any great extent at Nazareth because the people there did not trust him (6. 5) and in one of His sayings recorded in Matthew Jesus seems to have stipulated that there must be faith before He could heal (9. 29).

In these cases, however, what is meant is faith in Himself as Messiah, not co-operation with His healing power on the part of the patient. There was no possibility of such co-operation in the case of the dead son of the widow of Nain or of the other dead who were restored to life. Nor was it possible in the case of the centurion's servant (Luke 7. 2–10) or the daughter of the Syrophoenician woman (Mark 7. 24–30) both of whom were cured at a distance without Jesus having even seen them. If Jesus' miraculous power was therefore merely a matter of enabling patients to cure themselves, we must rule out not only the nature miracles but a number of well-authenticated healing miracles as well.

We are obviously moving here in a realm that we are only now beginning dimly to understand, involving the effect of mind upon body, especially the effect of the channelling of the healing power of God through minds attuned to God willing and praying for the restoration to health of unseen and unknown sufferers. The growing realization on the part of the Church of the fact of divine healing brought about through individuals or groups letting themselves be used by God for this purpose, helps us towards some understanding of the effect upon a sufferer when the channel is the selfless compassion of One who was Himself God's Son.

Some such sense that we are on the threshold of new discoveries, both in the field of psychosomatic medicine and in the Church's understanding of the healing power of prayer, which may lead us to a new conception of partnership between the doctor and the priest and between the nursing services and the congregations, must make us realize that any attempt to account for the healing miracles of Jesus under any categories of present-day psychiatry or medical practice is wholly unsatisfactory.

The chief impression that the miracles of Jesus in the realm of human suffering leave on our minds is that they were completely spontaneous, and that they happened almost inevitably as a result of some tremendous healing power that He possessed. His cures bear little resemblance to modern techniques in any sense. There was no thorough diagnosis, no long course of treatment, no period of convalescence. At a word or with a touch blind men received back their sight, lame men walked again, the dumb were able to speak, the paralysed recovered the use of their limbs, the dead were raised to life. Either we believe that these things happened or we make nonsense of the gospels. The only adequate explanation of the miracles lies in the last resort in the words of Jesus Himself: "If I by the finger of God cast out devils, then is the kingdom of God come upon you" (Luke 11. 20).

The Kingdom of God in Action

Jesus regarded His mission as twofold: to proclaim the Good News of the Kingdom and to heal the sick by casting out the demons that caused their maladies. He did not look upon His miracles as wonders. He refused to gratify the curiosity of the Pharisees by performing some supernatural trick (Mark 8. 12) for He had turned His back on that sort of thing at the Temptation. He regarded His miracles rather as 'signs' that the Reign of God on earth had really begun. Evil was being routed, disease and death were being defeated; the power of God, working through His Messiah, was proving stronger than the power of Satan.

The prophets had foretold that when the New Age dawned these were the very things that would happen (Isa. 61. 1; 35. 5–6). It has been well said that a miracle in the religious sense is not so much an inexplicable occurrence as an occurrence which brings an overwhelming sense of the very presence of God. And it was in this sense that the miracles of Jesus were regarded by the men of His day. Some new power had come into their midst; God was in action amongst them. In Jesus they saw "the finger of God" at work and they were certain that this strange power of the prophet from Nazareth came from Him.

What are we to say of the permanent value of the miracles? Is it enough to regard them merely as historical facts in the life of Jesus, part of the evidence that a New Age dawned when He walked in Galilee, or, conversely, acts that we should expect from such a unique personality as Jesus has been shown to be? St. John's Gospel suggests a deeper answer, and with those who find the miracles a stumbling-block when they are treated as historical incidents, perhaps it is one which finds a readier response.

The whole emphasis of the Fourth Gospel is on the eternal significance of Jesus. It is not so interested in the historical Jesus of Galilee and Jerusalem as in the Jesus of experience, the Jesus of the faith and worship of the early Church. So for the writer of the Fourth Gospel, the miracles have not so much a historical interest as a symbolical interest. They are the outward signs of deeper and eternal truth. This is far from being a contradiction of the picture presented in the synoptic gospels; it is on the contrary only making explicit what in them is implicit.

So for the Fourth Gospel and for us today the real significance of our Lord's feeding of the multitude (6. 1–14) is that Jesus is the Bread of Life—the guarantee of the only life that has meaning and substance which death cannot destroy, the sacrament of our heavenly home (6. 35, 41, 51–58). The healing of the man born blind (9. 1–12)—as indeed all of us are—means that for all mankind Jesus is the Light of the World, who brings into the bewilderment and perplexities of everyday existence the clarification of who we are, why we are here and what we may hope for (9. 5 cf. 8. 12). The raising of Lazarus (11. 1–44) has as its ultimate meaning the promise that Jesus is the pledge of Resurrection and Eternal Life for all who believe in Him (11. 25).

So in this deeper and indeed eternal sense Jesus is still working miracles wherever men and women who are spiritually blind, lame and paralysed, and even dead, are healed and restored by the power of His Spirit. "The physical miracles are external signs of the supreme messianic miracle, the rescue of men from the grip of the powers of evil—from sin. The supreme messianic miracle to which the miracles point is the salvation of men by the power of the living God exercised through the agency of the messiah."[1]

[1]Hoskyns & Davey: *The Riddle of the New Testament*, p. 120.

Chapter Twelve

THE LAST JOURNEY

CAESAREA Philippi, as we have noted earlier, marked the turning point in Jesus' ministry. In the earlier stage He seems to have thought, at times at least, that the message of the Kingdom of God, or the Kingdom of Heaven as it is called in Matthew, would spread like leaven in dough (Matt. 13. 33) or grow to vast proportions like the tiny seed of the mustard plant (Matt. 13. 31). In parables of this kind, suggesting the vast possibilities that lay ahead if men responded to the claims of God upon them, the permeation of the whole of life by a new spirit of dedication and power of renewal, Jesus indicated what would happen if men recognized that God reigned on earth as He did in heaven.

But in fact men did not respond. Jesus came up against the opposition that the prophets had encountered when they inveighed against luxury, greed, intolerance and extortion. The way was too hard for most. So it seems that Jesus took St. Peter's confession as a summons to a new policy. He would narrow the scope of His teaching ministry and concentrate on a small but sure foundation. In a sense this concentration on a few chosen disciples had been there all the time but it seems now to have a greater emphasis.

Jesus is bent on building the New Israel, with the twelve disciples representing the twelve tribes. His aim is to shape them by intensive instruction into a community which will fulfil Israel's highest vocation as expounded by Second Isaiah, the greatest of her prophets—that of the Servant who through suffering and sacrifice brings the world to the knowledge and service of God. So from Caesarea Philippi onwards Jesus' emphasis is all the time on the suffering that lies ahead and on the ignominious death which cannot have been far from His mind ever since His Baptism.

He is the Messiah, as St. Peter had rightly recognized, but His kingdom will not be won by might and power but by treading the path of sorrow. Jesus sets His face towards Jerusalem, the city of God's holy Temple, the religious centre of the land, the national shrine of old Israel, knowing that what awaits Him there is the certain death that will come as a result of the opposition that has been steadily increasing, fomented by the jealousy of the priests, the conservatism of the Pharisees and the sheer evil in human kind.

As the representative of the Kingdom of God Jesus must do battle with the Kingdom of Satan in the place where the old time prophets had shed their blood, for, as He said, "it cannot be that a prophet perish out of Jerusalem" (Luke 13. 33). He will go there not as the Son of David to found a political kingdom and rout the Roman oppressor but as the Son of Man who has chosen the role of the Servant, who reaches His triumph only through humiliation. Jesus invites His disciples to take up their crosses and follow Him, and He means this literally (Mark 8. 34), but in the event they cannot face the horror of crucifixion, and the Son of Man, as sole representative of the new people of God, goes to His death alone.

Peter's reaction to this unheard of conception of the Messiah's role is to protest with vigour. The idea of a suffering and dying Lord, even though this might be the necessary prelude to future glory as Jesus assured Him, was as repugnant to him as to anyone else. To Jesus, however, it was once more the voice of the Tempter with whom He had fought His battle after His Baptism. He had turned His back on short cuts to success then: He must do so still (Mark 8. 33).

The Transfiguration

The strange incident that happened a few days later, known as the Transfiguration of Jesus, is best described in St. Luke's account (9. 28–36). What had taken place at Caesarea

Philippi must have left the disciples in complete bewilderment. St. Peter as spokesman for them all had uttered the conviction that all of them must to some extent have shared. But at once Jesus had enjoined silence. His Messiahship must not be broadcast. It must remain a secret among them. This they might have understood since it was clear that the Master might have good reasons for avoiding a public disclosure at this particular juncture. What they could not understand, and could not, humanly speaking, be expected to understand, was His determination to court suffering and death, supremely confident that this was the will of God and that beyond the Cross lay the fulfilment of His destiny.

The Transfiguration, so far as they could comprehend it, and it is not certain that they grasped its full meaning, was to teach at least three of them that what Jesus had just said was true. The chosen three were the inner circle of the disciples, Peter, James and John. Jesus takes them on to a hill top, possibly among the foothills of Mt. Hermon, near Caesarea Philippi. While He prays the disciples fall asleep. On waking they see Jesus transformed with supernatural radiance, in the company of Moses and Elijah, with whom He speaks of His impending death. As Moses and Elijah are on the point of vanishing and Peter is trying to detain them, a dense cloud envelops the terrified disciples and a voice from the cloud says: "This is my beloved Son: hear him".

What are we to make of this extraordinary incident? It is impossible to disentangle history from theology as the story is told, and the actual circumstances surrounding this event can never be known. It cannot be dismissed as a hallucination though Luke's picture of the disciples as half-asleep suggests some kind of vision. This is more likely than that the story is a misplaced post-Resurrection appearance of Jesus. Physical transformation of the face as a result of intense spiritual experience is understandable, as in this case of Jesus after prolonged prayer, and the words of Peter as he seeks to make the vision permanent have a ring of actuality.

What is, however, quite clear is that through the Transfiguration of Jesus the disciples were not only being taught that the Master's incredible resolve to die is in accordance with the will of God but were also being given a foretaste of His future glory. Whatever happened it was for them an experience that corresponded with that of Jesus at His Baptism. They heard the voice of God confirming the Messiahship of Jesus and however little they may have understood it at the time they were being prepared to become preachers of His Resurrection.

The symbolism of the cloud which in Old Testament times represented the mysterious presence of God, the heavenly voice, the tabernacle, the high mountain and the reflection of the divine glory on the face of Jesus recall vividly the scene on Mt. Sinai when Moses communed with God and "wist not that his face shone". But St. Luke makes it explicit by using the very word "exodus" with reference to Jesus' death (9. 31). For this is the significance of the incident as the evangelist sees it. Jesus the new and greater Moses is about to embark upon the deliverance not merely of His own people from the bondage of Egypt but of mankind from the bondage of Satan by His Death and Resurrection in a new and greater Exodus. The twin pillars of the Old Testament dispensation, the Law and the Prophets, represented by Moses and Elijah in the vision, appear only to disappear and are replaced by the Messiah. Jesus is shown to be the sole Saviour of the New Israel. Almost as a token of that St. Luke records as His next action the healing of an epileptic boy (9. 37–43).

The Road to Jerusalem

It is significant that at this point both Mark and Luke introduce sayings of Jesus which are more radical than usual, in the direction of emphasizing both His own status (Mark 9. 38 ff.) and the cost of discipleship (Luke 9. 57 ff.; 14. 25–33). The crisis of Jesus' ministry is clearly at hand. It is difficult to trace the actual course of His journey to Jerusalem. Either He chose to take a devious route via Transjordan (Mark 10. 1) and

Jericho (Mark 10. 46) or else we are given in this part of the record reminiscences of other previous visits.

But throughout the long section in Luke which covers the journey (9. 51—19. 28) we get the impression of one set purpose underlying the whole narrative. "He steadfastly set his face to go to Jerusalem", "as they were on the way to Jerusalem", "he went on before going up to Jerusalem". Jerusalem is the goal and there is a new tenseness between Jesus and His followers. He does not walk with them but in front (Mark 10. 32). His conversation with them seems to have turned again and again to what was about to happen at Jerusalem. How little they understood can be seen from the request of James and John that they should have the places of honour in His Kingdom. Jesus, who saw His Kingdom coming by way of a Cross, told them that the way to places of honour in His Kingdom lay through service and sacrifice (Mark 10. 35-45).

How long this journey lasted it is impossible to say. It seems more likely, as Luke and John suggest, to have been more protracted than Mark would imply, perhaps lasting several months, the latter part of the period being spent in and around Jerusalem. It comes to an end, however, at the time of the Passover, i.e. probably in the spring of A.D. 29. This was the central festival of the Jewish year when pilgrims from all over the world flocked to Jerusalem and it would seem that this was the time chosen by Jesus to make His stand for the Kingdom. The Passover was the feast that commemorated the deliverance of the Jews from the bondage of a foreign power by the greater power of God. Jesus the Son of Man goes up to Jerusalem to defeat the power of evil by the same strong power of God.

One of the characteristic practices of the Old Testament prophets is known as prophetic symbolism. Ezekiel conducted a siege of Jerusalem in miniature with a sketch map of the city and toy engines of war (Ezek. 4. 1-3). In the splendid story of Micaiah ben-Imlah, one of the rival prophets dons a pair of iron horns with which he shows King Ahab how he will rout his Syrian enemies (1 Kings 22. 11). Jeremiah wears a yoke in public to indicate the coming supremacy of Babylon over Judah (Jer. 27. 2). In each of these cases the prophet thinks of himself as somehow identified with the purpose of Yahweh. He is not merely illustrating the event, he is helping it to happen.

In the last week of His ministry Jesus performed three symbolic actions of this kind. The first was His entry into Jerusalem on the Sunday before Good Friday, our Palm Sunday. On the previous day He had gone to lodge with His friends Martha, Mary and Lazarus at their house in Bethany near Jerusalem (John 12. 1) and there He remained until the Thursday of the following week. It was on the night of His arrival at Bethany that the indignation of at least one of the disciples was aroused by the action of Mary, whose highly sensitive character is commented on elsewhere in contrast to that of her efficient bustling sister Martha (Luke 10. 38–42). On this occasion she anointed His feet with costly fragrant ointment, an act which Jesus accepted as an anointing for His burial (John 12. 2–8).

The Triumphal Entry

He had other friends in the neighbourhood with whom He arranged for a donkey to be brought to Him at Bethany and it was in this manner that He made what is called His Triumphal Entry into Jerusalem. The purpose of this symbolic act is evident. The prophet Zechariah had claimed that when Messiah came to the Holy City He would not come as a conqueror on his war-horse, but "lowly, and riding upon an ass" as a Prince of Peace (Zech. 9. 9). Jesus by no means, as we have seen, accepted all that the Old Testament or popular belief associated with the coming of the Messiah but here was one strand of prophecy that accorded with His own conception of His role.

It is doubtful how many, if any, in the crowds who acclaimed Him as the Son of David, shouting Hosanna, God save Israel now, spreading their garments and strewing leaves in His path, knew what was in Jesus' mind. This time He did not disclaim the Messianic title, for He was demonstrating by

His action that He was indeed the Messiah coming to establish His Kingdom. But it was a far different Kingdom from that which the cheering mob expected. They may have been pilgrims coming up from Galilee who knew Jesus, or, as St. John suggests, the recent raising of Lazarus may have attracted the curiosity or enthusiasm of the Jerusalem people. For Jesus, however, it was no hour of triumph. St. Luke tells us that as He approached the city He wept over its blindness and foresaw its doom (19. 41 ff.).

Whatever was in Jesus' own mind such a symbolic entry into the city with its Messianic implications was bound to enrage the authorities, but at the same time to suggest caution in their reactions. That He was a dangerous innovator and presumptuous wonder-worker posing as the Messiah was obvious to them. Equally obvious was the conclusion that there was only one thing to be done with Him. The sole question was how and when. According to Mark, on that Palm Sunday night He entered the Temple, but merely looked around and returned to Bethany with the disciples (11. 11). Luke has probably preserved the sequence of events better when he records that when Jesus went into the Temple He at once set about driving out the hucksters. This seems a more suitable climax to the Triumphal Entry.

According to Mark, however, it was next day, on Monday of Holy Week that Jesus enacted this second piece of prophetic symbolism. On His way into the city there took place that odd incident of the cursing of the fig tree, so unlike the character of Jesus if it is taken as a historical incident, that we had best regard it as a corruption of a parable (Mark 11. 12–14, 20 ff. cf. Luke 13. 6–9). On reaching Jerusalem He went straight to the Temple.

The Temple was essentially a walled-in square consisting of a series of open-air courts centring on the Tabernacle, where the dark and solemn silence of the bare chapel called the Holy of Holies emphasized the mystery of the Presence of an invisible and undepictable God. Surrounding the Tabernacle were the various courts allocated to the priesthood, the laity and the women of Israel. The outermost court was that of the Gentiles who were debarred on pain of death from passing through it into the Israelite sector.

On the other hand the existence of an area reserved for Gentiles within the sacred precincts implied that they were included within the saving purposes of God and could become part of His people by embracing the Jewish faith and gaining access to the Court of Israel. Symbolically, the way to God was open to all, Jew and Gentile, but the Gentiles must approach Him by way of Israel, which meant in practice accepting the Old Testament and conforming to what the Law demanded of those who would claim to belong to His elect community.

The picture that the Court of the Gentiles presented when Jesus entered it, however, was more like that of an open-air market. The regulations governing the offering of sacrifices demanded that the cattle and birds should be certified free of any blemish. A clutter of stalls for the sale of such animals occupied the space intended for Gentile adherents and inquirers. Moreover, since the annual temple-tax obligatory on all Jews had to be paid in coinage approved by the Temple authorities, Jewish pilgrims had to exchange their local currency at bureaux installed for the purpose. All this traffic provided a considerable revenue for the priesthood.

The Cleansing of the Temple

The so-called Cleansing of the Temple which was carried out by Jesus at this point consisted in His deliberate overturning of these booths and tables, freeing the animals, scattering the money on the ground and driving the traders from the scene. What was the point of this? Clearly it had nothing to do with twentieth-century humanitarian concern for the sacrificial animals, nor, despite the mention in the Fourth Gospel of a "whip of cords" (John 2. 15), had it anything to do with the pros and cons of pacifism. It was not even a first-century religious reformation, since, as far as we know, business went on as usual the following day.

It was clearly a Messianic act. As the prophet Malachi had said (3. 1) "the Lord, whom ye seek, shall suddenly come to his temple". Now when He had come He had found corruption in the house of God, in its worship and in its priesthood. By this act of prophetic symbolism the Messiah in the name of God, and moved by righteous indignation, swept out the old religion lock, stock and barrel. It had become a travesty of what it was meant to be. What was intended to be "a house of prayer for all the nations" in the fine words of Isaiah 56. 7, said Jesus, had been turned into "a den of robbers" as Jeremiah long ago had pungently described it (7. 11).

Evil, greed and traffic in religiosity had poisoned the nation's life. The Gentiles were not only literally being pushed out of their rightful place in the sanctuary of God by the sordid money-grubbing of the religious leaders of the people, but symbolically also the world was being alienated from God by this sorry spectacle. A clean sweep must be made of this caricature of what the prophets had fought and died for. The old Kingdom of Satan which held sway even in this most holy place must make way for the new Kingdom of God.

It seems that from now until His Arrest Jesus was able to move about freely despite His violation of priestly privilege in the Temple. This action brought the Sadducees into unholy alliance with the Pharisees against Him, since not only were they outraged at the affront to their prestige, to say nothing of the challenge to their profits, but also the popular support that Jesus enjoyed threatened the security of their authority which rested not on the backing of the people but on that of the Roman government.

He came daily into Jerusalem from Bethany and there are various small incidents recorded of these days in which the conflict between Himself and the authorities has clearly become acute. He is challenged as to His right to interfere in Temple affairs (Mark 11. 27–33) and a more serious threat arises from an attempt to involve Him in a charge of treason against the Roman government on the question of the obligatory polltax (Mark 12. 13–17).

While Jesus is occupied in these last few days before His Arrest with controversy, public teaching and private instruction of the disciples, we may pause to look for a moment at the strange and enigmatic figure of Judas Iscariot. If Iscariot means 'the man from Kerioth' he was the only Judaean among the otherwise Galilean disciples. This most vilified of men will probably never be fathomed. The horror with which his betrayal of Jesus was regarded from the first tends to blind us to the fact that Jesus must at one time have thought him to be of apostolic calibre and had made him treasurer of the company.

Was he a disappointed enthusiast who had attached himself to Jesus as a potential political saviour and now felt himself to have been hoodwinked? Was he trying by his betrayal to force Jesus' hand and bring about the triumph of the Messiah he believed in by compelling Him to save Himself by some compelling demonstration of His power? Had he come at last to the conclusion that the religious authorities were right and that Jesus was a dangerous radical who threatened to destroy the hallowed traditions of the past? Or as the Fourth Gospel suggests (12. 4–6), was his motive plain greed?

At all events he consented to be the instrument of the Sadducees in betraying Jesus. Their difficulty was to lay hold of Him during the day when, as St. Luke tells us "the people all hung upon him, listening" (19. 48), whereas at night He lodged outside the city. Judas' bargain was that for thirty pieces of silver (Matt. 26. 15 cf. Zech. 11. 12), he would lead the officers of the authorities to Jesus conveniently at night, that he would identify Him for them and then let them take whatever action they chose.

Whether Judas clearly knew that this meant death for Jesus or not, Jesus Himself had no doubts. He had already also sensed Judas' intentions. It is against this background and with this knowledge that Jesus makes His arrangements for a last meal with His followers and at that Last Supper He enacts His third piece of prophetic symbolism in Holy Week.

Chapter Thirteen

THE TRIAL AND DEATH OF JESUS

IN making arrangements to hold the Last Supper it seems as if Jesus had planned beforehand as in the case of the Triumphal Entry. A room had been reserved in a friend's house—probably the home of Mary, the mother of John Mark, which was later to become the meeting place of the Christian community in Jerusalem after the Crucifixion (Acts 12. 12)—and two of the disciples were sent in from Bethany on the Thursday to complete the preparations (Mark 14. 12 ff.). The mysterious nature of the instructions given to the two disciples—to look for and follow a man bearing a pitcher of water, in a country where women were normally the water carriers—would seem to indicate a desire for secrecy.

There is much discussion as to whether the meal Jesus and the apostles ate together was the Jewish Passover or a pre-Passover occasion. The difficulty arises when we try to square Mark's chronology of Holy Week with that given in the Fourth Gospel. Mark appears to suggest that the Last Supper was a celebration of the Passover held on the Thursday evening, and that Jesus was arrested, tried and crucified between then and Friday evening. This haste would not be impossible but the Fourth Gospel claims that the Passover was not held until after the Crucifixion (John 18. 28).

Recent evidence would seem to suggest that Mark is compressing his narrative of Holy Week as he has already compressed the record of Jesus' ministry in and around Jerusalem. It now appears that there may have been an official Passover celebration after the Crucifixion on Good Friday, that referred to by St. John, and an unofficial Passover held by some religious bodies on the Tuesday evening, that referred to in

Mark's compressed narrative. This would make the Trial of Jesus more like what one would expect, since He appears before four separate judges, and a space of three days between His Arrest on the Tuesday and His Crucifixion on the Friday would allow for this better than a space of approximately twelve hours. However, the problem is complicated and this solution has its own difficulties. It is therefore wiser to stick to the traditional order of events as given by St. Mark and leave the question open as to whether the Last Supper was in fact a Passover meal.

If it was not a proper Passover that was celebrated on that momentous occasion it had more than a Passover significance. Up to a point it must have been the same kind of common meal which Jesus had eaten with His disciples on many occasions. But there was in the minds of all of them a sense of finality which was heightened when Jesus told them that He knew that one of them was about to betray Him (Mark 14. 18).

At the end of the meal He enacted the third piece of symbolism in Holy Week by taking the bread, blessing it and handing it to them saying: "This is my body." Then similarly, blessing the cup of wine, He gave it to them saying: "This is my blood of the new covenant which is shed for many." St. John includes at this meal the impressive scene where Jesus washes the disciples' feet as an object lesson in service (John 13. 1–14) and follows it with a discourse by Jesus (chs. 14–17) which contains perhaps the most sublime teaching in the gospels.

But our interest centres for the moment on the words of Jesus as He broke the bread and gave the cup to His disciples, an action which as St. Paul tells us was among the earliest traditions to be handed on to converts to the new Christian faith (1 Cor. 11. 23 ff.) and which is still at the heart of the chief sacrament of the Church. What did Jesus mean by these words? He knows that He is going to His death not because Judas has betrayed Him or because the ecclesiastics have conspired against Him but because His death is an essential part of His work on earth.

146

Only by His death can the Reign of God come, as He says, "with power" (Mark 9. 1). The Son of Man, who is conscious of His divine status, who had trodden the path of the Servant of God and identified Himself completely with mankind, must go through to the last act of humiliation and drink the cup of bitterness to the full. Like the Servant whom Isaiah depicted (Isa. 53) He must perform the last and greatest act of service by laying down His life for His friends (John 15. 13).

As He prepares to make this sacrifice in which He clearly offers Himself on behalf of the new community which He has founded, He enacts it before them in the prophetic manner by breaking bread and giving it to them, and by passing a loving-cup, as symbols of His Body and Blood. His death is to be a new covenant between God and Israel (Ex. 24. 8). In modern terms, Jesus is proclaiming that through Him a new relationship is now possible between God and the new Israel, a new order, a fresh start for mankind. At that moment the new community was represented by these eleven timid mortals and a twelfth who was on the point of betraying Him, but such was Jesus' faith in God that He believed that out of this sorry handful His Father would yet create the fellowship He had designed to reshape the life of the world.

Gethsemane

Just at the foot of the Mount of Olives there is to this day a little walled plantation of ancient and gnarled trees. It is the Garden of Gethsemane, a name that evokes all the horror of the Crucifixion even more than the Cross itself. It was to this place that Jesus led His disciples after the Last Supper and it was here perhaps that He fought the biggest battle of all. The darkness of the night, the exhaustion of the disciples and the mental agony of Jesus combine to make a sombre picture. Little wonder that His soul was "exceeding sorrowful even unto death" (Mark 14. 34).

It was as if the whole Power of evil rose up there to confront Him: the hostility of His own townsmen, the bitterness of the

Pharisees, the vindictiveness of the Sadducees, the faithlessness of His followers, the cowardice of His disciples, one of whom was on His way to betray Him. Yet these were on the whole decent citizens, many of them deeply religious, most of them well-intentioned. It is the whole tragedy of the human situation that shatters Jesus—the prejudice, bigotry, malevolence and weakness of ordinary human nature. So the servants of goodness and truth had always been received. The prophets had found it so and now the Messiah went down into the abyss for the men He came to save.

Jesus' horror when He prays: "Remove this cup from me" (Mark 14. 36) is not merely a prayer to be spared the agony of drinking the bitter potion of a horrible death, but rather the revulsion of perfect goodness against the thought of the depths to which evil could drive mankind. But even here the human impulse is quickly followed by the supreme act of obedience: "Nevertheless not my will but thy will be done." If it is the Father's will, as Jesus believes it to be, that the Son should drink the cup of humiliation to the dregs, so be it.

Thus it is with complete composure that Jesus awaits His Arrest, a composure which He maintains throughout His Trial. Shortly there descends upon the silence of Gethsemane the sound of hurrying feet, the muttering of distant voices, and in the flickering light of torches the guardians of religious purity and their armed police escort lay hold of Jesus. The Judas-kiss which betrayed Him is matched by the action of the other eleven who flee for their lives. It is at this point that the revealing and wholly irrelevant comment of Mark (14. 51–52) on the young man who fled naked from the scene suggests that we have here a first-hand witness of the whole incident and perhaps of many other events in Passion Week.

The Trial of Jesus

Jesus is haled off for His Trial and before it is over He has had to appear before four different judges—Annas, Caiaphas, Herod and Pilate. As we read the narrative, however, it is clear that it is not Jesus who is being tried but His judges. The formal verdict of guilty is passed on the prisoner but the dignity and majesty of Jesus are nowhere so plainly seen as in the simple and restrained story of how He faced His accusers, and nowhere are the vindictiveness, prejudice and weakness of ordinary men revealed more patently than in the bearing of His judges.

For an account of the Trial we must supplement St. Mark's gospel by reference to the other three. St. John tells us that the *First Trial*, a preliminary examination, took place before Annas, the father-in-law of Caiaphas. He was no longer high priest but he was still the leader of the Sadducean party and the power behind the scenes. This possibly took place in Annas' own house and was probably held before midnight.

Nothing of note emerged from this informal trial except that either in the courtyard of Annas' house or in the official residence of Caiaphas, to which Jesus was next sent (both may of course have been part of the same building) there occurred the second great betrayal by a disciple. This time it was Peter himself, who with another of the apostles, probably John, had plucked up enough courage to come back to the scene and now swore to high heaven that he had never had anything to do with Jesus. The crowing of the cock that heralded a new day reminded him of Jesus' words the evening before (Mark 14. 30) but more shattering still was the look from the Master that said more than words (Luke 22. 61).

The *Second Trial* took place just after daybreak on the Friday morning in the official residence of Joseph Caiaphas, the high priest. The Sanhedrin had been hurriedly summoned and indeed the whole series of trials is conducted in an atmosphere of haste to get the business over before the official Passover. How far the procedure was irregular or the trial illegal we cannot now say. This second trial was marked by the lack of clear evidence and by the refusal of Jesus to refute the charges. The climax, however, was reached when Caiaphas asked Him point blank to say whether He was the Messiah or no. To this

Jesus replied for the first time openly that He was, and added words which confirmed what was in the high priest's mind self-confessed blasphemy, namely that His destiny was on the point of being fulfilled and that His judges would themselves see it (Mark 14. 59–62).

This was enough for Caiaphas and the rest, and the Sanhedrin condemned Jesus to death. It is difficult to see how they could have done anything else unless they had admitted that He was in fact the Messiah. The Sanhedrin had, however, no power to carry out the death sentence. Only the Roman authorities could do that. So Jesus was taken for His *Third Trial* to the Praetorium, the headquarters of the Roman Procurator when he visited Jerusalem, which he did especially when there was a danger of religious riots, and where in this case Pontius Pilate was installed for the Passover celebrations. This trial was of course the one that mattered. Here it was a case of life or death.

On general Roman principles Pilate would not be willing to condemn a man to death on religious grounds. On the other hand his reputation in Rome was not good: he had been in trouble before and he dared not risk opposing the will of the Jewish leaders. The charge brought against Jesus (Luke 23. 2) was threefold: (1) that He was an agitator, (2) that He had encouraged people not to pay their taxes to Rome and (3) that He called Himself King of the Jews. Pilate conducted the case inside the building while the Jews who were not allowed for religious reasons to enter a pagan edifice at Passover waited outside.

At one point it transpired that Jesus was a Galilean and Pilate promptly sent him to the tetrarch of Galilee, Herod Antipas, son of Herod the Great, who was in Jerusalem at the time. This *Fourth Trial* was a farce (Luke 23. 5–12). There was no semblance of judicial investigation. Herod regarded Jesus as a curiosity and a miracle-monger. When he could get no amusement from Him he handed Him over to the soldiers who entered into the spirit of the game and sent the "King of the Jews" back to Pilate dressed in royal attire. Luke's brief account is presumably a parallel to the mockery of Jesus by the Roman soldiers in the other three gospels. What they probably did was to drape one of their scarlet military cloaks about Him, place a chaplet of thorns on His brow in imitation of the laurel wreaths of the Roman emperors, put a reed in His hand to act as a sceptre, and give a Roman military salute with uplifted arm in mockery of the Jewish Caesar.

Pilate, it would appear, was unwilling to condemn Jesus. Patently He was innocent. St. Matthew's gospel suggests that a dream of Pilate's wife may have had something to do with his reluctance to accede to the priests' demands. He sought a way out by offering to release Jesus as an act of clemency, an old custom at the great festivals. Meantime a crowd of supporters of one Barabbas, a popular rebel under sentence of death for murder and rioting, had come to ask that the Procurator's pardon should be bestowed upon him. Some ancient manuscripts give this man's name as Jesus Barabbas, in which case Pilate offered the Jews the alternative of releasing Jesus Barabbas or Jesus who is called the Christ. The priests persuaded the mob that the way to secure the liberation of Barabbas was to force Pilate to crucify Jesus. So the cry went up outside the Praetorium: Release Barabbas; Crucify Jesus. Pilate literally washed his hands of the whole business (Matt. 27. 24) and handed Jesus over to be scourged and crucified.

The Crucifixion

Crucifixion was a most horrible death. Small wonder that the disciples fled. The criminal was beaten almost lifeless. Then he had to carry the crossbar to the place of execution, where his hands and feet were nailed to the beams. Jesus was physically so exhausted by the rough treatment of the various trials (cf. Mark 14. 65; 15. 16 ff.) and by the scourging, that a passer-by, one Simon, probably a pilgrim from Cyrene in North Africa, was forced to carry His Cross for Him.

The way from the Praetorium led along what is now known

as the Via Dolorosa to a spot then outside the city walls, but now inside the Church of the Holy Sepulchre, known as Golgotha, for which the Vulgate name is Calvary. There at nine o'clock on Good Friday morning, the third hour, Jesus was crucified between two criminals. As was the normal practice a board was placed on the Cross, giving the reason for execution. In Jesus' case it bore the words: "The King of the Jews," a jibe of Pilate at the people he loathed.

The wealthy women of Jerusalem had a pious custom of attending public executions and offering the victims on their crosses drugged wine to deaden the pain. This Jesus refused. At a crucifixion the cross was a low erection. The head of the dying man was only eighteen inches above the bystanders. Jesus was thus both able to hear the sneers of those who passed along the road nearby, and also to be heard by the women who stood near the Cross (John 19. 25). Between them the gospels record seven sayings from the Cross: read progressively as a commentary on Jesus' experience they are overpoweringly moving. There is first the word of forgiveness for those who have brought Him to His death: "Father, forgive them, for they know not what they do"; then the word of hope for the penitent thief: "Today shalt thou be with me in Paradise"; His care for those who were left sorrowing, His Mother and St. John, as He commended them to one another: "Woman, behold thy son!" and "Behold thy mother"; the momentary sense of dereliction: "My God, my God, why hast thou forsaken me?"; the sheer physical agony: "I thirst"; His task accomplished: "It is finished"; and His final commitment of Himself to God: "Father, into thy hands I commend my spirit."

At three o'clock in the afternoon Jesus died, much sooner than was the case with most crucified victims who sometimes died slowly for days. When the soldiers came to break the legs of the three men on the crosses, to hasten their death so that the bodies might be removed before the Passover, they found Jesus dead. One of them to make certain jabbed His side with his spear (John 19. 34). It seems that Jesus' death coincided with an earthquake, a sirocco, or both. The synoptists record that from twelve to three there was darkness over the land and that the Temple curtain was torn in two.

The last rites were performed by a wealthy member of the Sanhedrin who voted against the condemnation of Jesus, Joseph of Arimathaea, who asked Pilate's permission to remove the body of Jesus from the Cross, took it down and wrapped it in burial clothes, laying it in a nearby tomb in the rock, and rolling the normal cartwheel stone along its groove to cover the mouth of the vault.

Some of the women who had been at the Crucifixion followed Jesus to the end. St. John adds that Nicodemus who had come to Jesus secretly by night (John 3. 1–2) was also there and St. Matthew adds that the Pharisees, fearing some trick by the disciples, put a seal on the stone (Matt. 27. 62–66).

Beyond the Cross

We have already considered the evidence for the Resurrection in Chapter Six. To use an Irishism, if the gospels had ended with the Crucifixion they would never have been written. A crucified Messiah was so complete a travesty of all that had ever been hoped for and promised of Him that Jesus' claim to be what the prophets had foretold would never have been countenanced for a week, let alone two thousand years, if the Cross had been the end.

The Christian Church was not founded on the teaching of Jesus. It was founded by men who believed that the Jesus whom they had forsaken to go to His Death alone had risen from the grave, triumphant over death, that He had appeared to many of them, and thereby had turned the Cross from being a symbol of shame and defeat into a gateway to victory and glory. Not only was the Church founded on this belief but the whole of the New Testament was written as a result of it.

If the Resurrection had not been the starting point of faith, not a word of gospels or epistles would ever have been added to the Old Testament. Christianity might have flourished for a space, though even this is doubtful, as a Jewish sect cherishing the memory of a great but deluded teacher, before gradually disintegrating and finally disappearing. But the fact of history is that this did not happen.

The fact of history is, firstly, that a band of men on the night of the Crucifixion were nowhere to be seen. They were hiding in terror of their lives and in utter disillusionment. They had been followers of a beloved Master in whom they had trusted, in whom they had recognized a unique personality, and from whom power that could only come from God had streamed so strongly that they felt that no ordinary human title of honour would fit Him, but that He must be none other than the heaven-sent Messiah. All this had come tumbling to the ground. Hope, faith and confidence had been shattered as their Lord was mocked and beaten, tortured and killed.

And the fact of history is, secondly, that these same men a few days later were cock-a-hoop, jubilant and triumphant, and that a few weeks later they had embarked on the task of converting the world. Life and the future had changed overnight. Their beloved Master was after all stronger than death, stronger than the evil that had crucified Him. He had risen from the dead, He had appeared to them, they had seen Him, they had talked with Him. Now they began to understand better the meaning of these dark sayings which had always perplexed them—His words about His Death being only the prelude to greater Life, His prophecies about His future glory and exaltation, His reference to the Kingdom coming "with power".

It is not too much to say that the whole validity of the Christian religion turns on the fact of the Resurrection. If Jesus was wrong in His belief that the Cross was only the beginning and not the end, we have no right to give to anything He said a status higher than the words of a deluded martyr. Creeds, Church and Bible become a nonsense. More than that, if the Resurrection is not true it means that not only

Christianity but any view of life except utter pessimism or Bertrand Russell's "unyielding despair" is impossible. For this would mean that what is by common consent the most morally perfect human life of which we have any record could be snuffed out for ever by prejudice, stupidity and malice. If this is so, hope, faith and charity as well as beauty, goodness and truth become bereft of all meaning.

The story of the Ascension which is recorded in any detail only at the beginning of the book of Acts (1. 1–11) is best regarded as a pictorial representation of the fact that after a time the appearances of the Risen Christ ceased. The disciples knew that as He had told them the Son of Man was now exalted in power and glory, freed from the limitations of an earthly body, yet with His Church "alway even unto the end of the world" (Matt. 28. 20). Jesus was indeed with them in a more vital sense than He had ever been in Galilee, and it was from that communion with Him that the real history of the Church began.

Chapter Fourteen

A NEW PATTERN OF LIFE

THE fundamental truth that Jesus proclaimed is, as we have seen, that the Rule of God had begun on earth—the New Age had dawned. Signs of it were evident on every hand. Men were being healed of their sicknesses, sinners were being forgiven; disease and evil were being routed by this new out-pouring of the Spirit of God through Jesus Himself. The Rule of Satan, by which everyone knew that Jesus meant the triumph of evil in all its forms, including disease, madness and death, was being broken by a stronger power than Satan.

God was in their midst, presenting them with a challenge through the words and works of Jesus either to enter His Kingdom or to remain outside. To stay outside was easy. The gate that led to destruction was wide and the road was broad. To enter the Kingdom was the most demanding de-cision a man could be faced with. The gate was narrow and the path was small. But it led to the only thing that was worth while in the whole world—life (Matt. 7. 13-14). The man who entered the Kingdom of God, who put himself under the Rule of God, obtained the one priceless possession—life in all its fulness, life as it was meant to be, life that had an eternal quality in it (John 10. 10).

When in St. John's gospel Jesus talks so frequently of eternal life He does not mean some remote life beyond the grave but life here and now lived in such a relationship to God that death becomes not a terminus but a gateway to something better (10. 28; 17. 3). He means precisely the same thing when He talks of the Kingdom of God so far as it affects ordinary men and women. To take the great step of entering the Kingdom is to step into life eternal here and now.

What then was the condition of entering the Kingdom that made it so hard and found so very few willing to face it? The answer as Jesus gives it is once again the same in the Fourth Gospel as in the synoptics. To Nicodemus He says, You must be born again (John 3. 3); to the disciples He says, You must become like little children (Mark 10. 15). In order to enter the Kingdom a man must strip himself of all his pride and vanity, his self-sufficiency and self-righteousness, and with the trustfulness of a little child, with a child's sense of its own helplessness, turn to God, as to a Father, acknowledging Him as his Creator and Preserver.

This is what Jesus means by repentance (Mark 1. 15). Not that men should express formal regret for their past offences or even be genuinely sorry about their failure to live up to their best intentions, but that there should be a complete revolution of the whole personality, a change of direction and policy, a turning of the back upon the natural tendencies towards self-preservation, self-enrichment, self-glorification, towards egocentricity in every form, and a turning of the face towards God. The life of a citizen of the Kingdom is God-centred, not self-centred. The act of repentance means commitment of the whole self to God, including identification of the human will with the will of God, so that a man's own purposes for himself cease to matter since his whole concern is that God's purpose should prevail (cf. Matt. 10. 39).

What then brings a man to the knowledge that he needs to repent? The answer is, his encounter with Jesus Himself. In Jesus he meets God. In His teaching, in His ministry, God is speaking and acting. What Jesus says He says not from Himself but from God (John 14. 24); what He does is done not by Himself but by God (John 5. 36). God is in history, in the human life of Jesus, confronting men with a challenge and an invitation. Jesus reveals God as the Father whose mercy and love open the door of the Kingdom to men as they are, sinful, foolish and perplexed, if they will only, like the Prodigal Son, see their sin and folly and ask forgiveness (Luke 15. 17–18).

It is in the light of this overruling idea of the Kingdom of God that Jesus' teaching is to be regarded. As the Kingdom of God is a new order, involving a new kind of life, there must be a new design for living, a new pattern of life for new men. Now it follows from the nature of life in the Kingdom that what Jesus gives is not a set of rules, because no amount of mechanical observance of rules could ever achieve what is the essence of the new life, namely a spontaneous response of gratitude to God for His act of love in offering a fresh start to harassed and fear-ridden mortals. Life for the citizen of the Kingdom is essentially a personal relationship to God. So the teaching of Jesus is better described in T. W. Manson's words, as "a compass rather than an ordnance map". It is something that gives the general direction to be followed but each man has to pick his own steps.

We have seen too that in the course of His ministry in Galilee Jesus' views changed. His first proclamation of the Kingdom of God was for all. The crowds who flocked to hear Him and made the synagogues too small were all potentially citizens of the new Kingdom. The net was cast wide (Matt. 13. 47) but what it drew in was mostly worthless. This was not the kind of Kingdom people wanted to hear about, least of all the upholders of the Law and their sympathizers. So the crowds thinned because the things that Jesus emphasized as necessary for life in the Kingdom were the things people found most difficult. Jesus' audiences left Him because then as now their greed and laziness and selfishness were stronger than their desire to enter the Kingdom. They saw the light and preferred darkness (John 3. 19).

So it became clear to Him that the Kingdom must be built on a solid nucleus, on the rock-like Peter (Matt. 16. 18) and his companions who had, even if only dimly, grasped the true nature of Jesus' message. They may not have understood it all but they agreed that there was no other place for them apart from Jesus (John 6. 68). It was to the disciples then, the Twelve and other close followers, the first men to glimpse something of the real nature of the new age, that Jesus addressed most of His teaching. To the crowds He had preferred to speak in parables, homely, simple stories illustrating one or other facet of His message. The disciples were however the first members of the new community which Jesus intended to build. To them He disclosed "the secret of the Kingdom of God" (Mark 4. 11).

Mark's account of the life of Jesus contains, as we know, little or no teaching. The document Q—the collection of sayings of Jesus—was used principally by Matthew and Luke. Luke distributes the teaching of Jesus through his whole narrative. Matthew on the other hand plans his gospel in five sections, each consisting of narrative followed by discourse. Clearly this arrangement is designed to suggest a parallel between the five books of the Law of Moses and the five books of the Law of Christ. Matthew is not concerned with the chronological order of Jesus' teaching but is bent on grouping it together in accordance with subject matter, whether it comes from Q, Mark or elsewhere.

The advantage from our point of view, however, is that it gives us in readily accessible form an insight into the mind of Jesus as He deals in these five discourses with the great themes that formed the subject of His teaching. By far the most important of these is the Sermon on the Mount, which occupies chapters 5–7. The others deal with the missionary vocation of the Church (ch. 10), the meaning of the Kingdom (ch. 13), Christian behaviour (ch. 18) and God's judgment of the world (chs. 24–25). In all cases we may be sure that what we are being given is only a selection of the kind of things Jesus said. The small and fragmentary collection of sayings that have found their way into the gospels is neither a comprehensive system of theology or ethics nor can it possibly represent more than a fraction of the things Jesus said.

What we have in the so-called Sermon on the Mount is unlikely to have been originally a single sermon delivered in any particular place, but is rather a collection of the best known, best remembered and therefore probably most often repeated sayings of Jesus brought together and given the form of a sermon. It is at all events enough to give us a clear idea of Jesus' design for living in the new age for those who had entered the Kingdom. Its solemn introduction (5. 1–2) underlines the fact that it was the avowed intention of Jesus to provide a new Law for the new age. Until then old Israel had lived under the terms and obligations of the Law of Moses. That was not only the law of the land, it was the law of life: religion, morality and good citizenship rolled into one.

Now a new and greater Moses, likewise on a 'mountain', sets up a pattern of living which is to replace the Mosaic law in the life of the new Israel, not in contradiction of the old law but in fulfilment, completion and transcendence of it. The new Law does not abrogate the old Law. It lifts it on to a higher plane. "All the prophets and the law prophesied until John" (Matt. 11. 13)—the old order reigned until then—but now there is new wine and it must have new bottles (Mark 2. 22).

The Beatitudes

If the Sermon on the Mount may be said to contain the essence of Jesus' teaching, the Beatitudes, with which it opens (5. 3–12), take us right to the heart of it. These eight short, crisp and memorable utterances of our Lord put in a nutshell what it means to be a Christian.

(1) "Blessed are the poor in spirit, for theirs is the kingdom of heaven." The "poor in spirit" are those who live in complete dependence on God, who have committed their lives wholly to Him, who are deeply conscious of their own inadequacy and constant failure to measure up to God's standards. These, says Jesus, are already in the Kingdom of God, or, as Matthew calls it out of reverent aversion to frequent use of the sacred name, the Kingdom of Heaven. They are, that is, in the right relationship to God.

(2) "Blessed are they that mourn: for they shall be comforted." The Psalmist had said: "Because they have no changes, therefore they fear not God" (Ps. 55. 19). Jesus goes further and says that it is through tears and sorrow that we come closest to God. It may be the sorrow of a broken heart, or of a deep compassion for the plight of mankind, or it may be the contrition of the penitent. All of them are the exact opposite of complacency, indifference to the needs of others and self-satisfaction. The promise of Jesus is that God comforts, encourages, uplifts and strengthens those to whom deep love brings deep sorrow.

(3) "Gentle Jesus, meek and mild" conjures up a picture of Christ which most people would rightly regard as a travesty of the truth. It was not meekness or mildness in the modern sense of the words which characterized a Jesus who could on occasion be angry and even violent (Mark 3. 5; 11. 15) and who minced no words in denouncing insincerity and hypocrisy (Mark 7. 6). When Jesus says: "Blessed are the meek", therefore, He does not mean "blessed are the spineless, effeminate and ineffectual". The best definition of the biblical word is probably as William Barclay says: "God-controlled". The citizen of the Kingdom who looks to the life of Jesus to find what 'meekness' means, finds there no wish-washy, colourless doormat, as the word now tends to imply, but a powerful, purposeful Figure whose perfect obedience to the will of God involved compassion, sympathy and tenderness but also, on occasion, indignation, condemnation and resistance. Only the man who is God-controlled is master of his fate and captain of his soul, or as the Bible puts it, "the meek shall inherit the earth".

(4) The fourth Beatitude commends those who "hunger and thirst after righteousness", and once again we are saddled with a word, "righteousness", which has an unpleasant sound for modern ears. We cannot forget its association with 'self-righteousness' which significantly enough is how we have mostly come to regard it. J. B. Phillips suggests instead

161

'goodness', and the New English Bible translates the sentence: "How blest are those who hunger and thirst to see right prevail (or to do what is right)." Any of these brings us much closer to what was in Jesus' mind. For famine- and drought-stricken Palestinian peasants food and drink were no casual or relative desires as they are in an affluent society but stark and absorbing necessities. So the man on whom Jesus sets the seal of His approval is the man who is passionately concerned that justice should always be done, that wrongs should always be righted, and, for himself, that he should always do the right thing.

(5) The teaching of Jesus is, as we might expect, rooted in the faith and practice of the Old Testament. There is no word there which is more used to characterize God than the word which in the next Beatitude is translated 'mercy'. But in the Old Testament it means more than the modern sense of letting a person off lightly or giving him the benefit of the doubt. It is rather 'loving-kindness' or 'faithful love', it is the attitude which God adopts towards the people to whom He is bound in covenant relationship. It is because they know that this is what God is like that His people, as in the psalms, have every reason for confidence and thankfulness. "Blessed are the merciful, for they shall obtain mercy" is Jesus' summons to those who would be His followers to match God's love to man with a like love for one another. This means sheer un-grudging readiness to understand, tolerate and forgive others as God Himself does to us. Without such a readiness we cannot be at one with God.

(6) "Blessed are the pure in heart, for they shall see God" is perhaps the most daunting of the Beatitudes. Who can hope to fulfil this condition any more than that of the psalmist: "Who shall ascend into the hill of the Lord? And who shall stand in his holy place? He that hath clean hands and a pure heart; who hath not lifted up his soul unto vanity, and hath not sworn deceitfully." (Ps. 24. 3–4). What act of charity, devotion or sacrifice is ever done without an element of calcu-

lation; when is love ever free from self-interest? Yet according to Jesus, purity of heart is the only way to the vision of God. The most that any man alive can hope for is to begin to eliminate, consciously in part but much more by laying himself open to the Spirit of God in prayer and sacrament, the hate, jealousy, greed, lust, vanity and other evils which Jesus lists elsewhere as the things that stand between us and purity of heart (Mark 7. 20–23). As he does so he comes that much nearer to the full knowledge of God which can only be experienced hereafter.

(7) Perhaps the best one-word description of the task of the Christian is reconciliation, the breaking down of the barriers that divide man from man as Christ has broken down the barrier that separated man from God. As St. Theresa has put it, we are Christ's hands and feet to do His bidding. This is what is meant by the seventh Beatitude: "Blessed are the peacemakers, for they shall be called the sons of God." "Sons of God" in the biblical sense means sharing the character of God, doing the things God does. A man is behaving like God if he is active in promoting the wellbeing of the community in every possible way, for the word 'peace-making' in the biblical sense means just that. It is more than trying to settle private quarrels, to pour oil on troubled waters, or to assist the cause of world peace, although these are all part of it. Wherever there is hardship, need, suffering, injustice, discrimination, there can be no peace in the biblical sense, for this implies life in the right relationship to God and to one another. This Beatitude confers Christ's accolade on the social worker, the reformer, the politician, the statesman, the Trade Union official, the doctor, the nurse, and the unnamed host of unprofessional men and women of goodwill who help to promote the welfare of others.

(8) The last Beatitude is a corollary of its predecessor. It proclaims the blessing of God upon those who have been "persecuted for righteousness' sake" and links them with the prophets of Israel who suffered the same fate. Any man who

is not content with things as they are, in Church or State, and who tries to bring about reforms is open to misunderstanding, misrepresentation and sometimes persecution. Jesus had no illusions that the path of His followers would be strewn with roses. His words have come true in the experience of the early Christians, at the Reformation and in recent times. The life of the Church has been renewed again and again by the sacrifice of those who have been martyred for their faith. But the Beatitude does not limit the blessing of God to those who win a martyr's crown. It includes those who suffer 'insults' and 'slander' in their fight for what is right. This is the hallmark of the true servant of God.

The Letter and the Spirit

Jesus then sums up in homely illustrations the role of Christians in the world. They are to be the salt which gives the right flavour to society, and they can do this only if they retain their distinctive characteristics. They are to be like Christ Himself, the light of the world (John 8. 12), illuminating its darkness by their example of charity and care for others. This is how men will be drawn into the service of God. Every Christian is to be an advertisement for Christ (5. 13–16).

It was no part of the intention of Jesus to dismiss the revelation of the will of God that had been handed down in the Old Testament. We have already seen that He went straight to the heart of the hopes and prayers of prophets and psalmists as they looked for the coming of God's Messiah. From all that they had to say He singled out what seemed to Him to be the essence of the truth they had been inspired to proclaim, and left on one side what He deemed to have outlived its purpose.

So in making plain His attitude to the legacy of the Law, He insists that His followers should not discard the well-tried guides to conduct that had been handed down through the centuries but that they should lift them on to a higher plane than was the practice of the religious authorities of His day.

164

The Pharisees made a fetish of mechanical observance and literal compliance with the minutiae of laws and traditions that had outlived their usefulness. Jesus claimed the right to establish priorities and to command obedience to the spirit of the Law rather than to the letter of the Law. Far from being a less demanding standard of behaviour than that of punctilious observance of every detail of a written code, the new interpretation that Jesus offered was, He claimed, far more exacting (5. 17–20).

Jesus' high-handed attitude to the Law on such questions as the Sabbath, fasting, and mixing with "publicans and sinners" (Mark 2. 27; 2. 18; 2. 16) might on the face of it suggest that life for His followers would be easier than for the painstaking Pharisee who had no such dispensations. But here, in the Sermon on the Mount, He shows by taking examples chiefly from the Ten Commandments that to live up to the spirit of the Law is far more difficult than to observe it to the letter (5. 21–48).

The man who takes the Beatitudes seriously and recognizes that the Christian life is primarily a matter not of rules but of relationships, will not be content with himself if he refrains from the actual act of murder, which is forbidden in the sixth commandment. Jesus insists that murder has in effect been committed if uncontrolled anger and hatred poison a man's mind and fill his heart with murderous intent. He may escape the judgment of a court of law but he will not escape the judgment of God. Similarly the seventh commandment forbids adultery, meaning by that any extra-marital sexual intercourse. Elsewhere Jesus insists on marriage as part of God's natural order, implicit in His creation of men and women. Marriage is meant to be life-long and indissoluble (Mark 10. 2–12). Here He not only condemns legal divorce and sex outside marriage which may lead to it, but points again to the inward disposition. To cultivate lustful thoughts and intentions is tantamount to infidelity. The third commandment forbade the breaking of a legal oath solemnly taken in the name of God. Jesus insists that the real sin consists not in the formal act of perjury but in being the kind of person whose word cannot be trusted.

Perhaps no saying of Jesus has been so much misunderstood as the next injunction "to turn the other cheek". It has been used as an argument for pacifism, and the Church has been castigated for its hypocrisy in countenancing war in blatant defiance of this precept. On the other hand the saying has been used to illustrate the sheer futility and impracticability of taking the teaching of Jesus seriously. In either case the words are wrested from their context. Firstly, Jesus is discussing individual behaviour on the part of committed Christians, not the national interests of nominally Christian or anti-Christian states which have to cope with the complexities and compromises of political action. Secondly, Jesus is not telling us what we should do when we are attacked by a foreign power or even by an armed bandit. It might be expedient in either case not to retaliate but there would be nothing specifically Christian in such behaviour.

Jesus is once again stressing the importance of having the right disposition. The old principle was "an eye for an eye and a tooth for a tooth"—"give as good as you get". The new law of Christ demands that we go to any lengths to effect reconciliation. It may involve putting up with personal insults, i.e. "turning the other cheek", meeting our opponent more than half-way, swallowing our pride. In all cases it is the opposite of weak-kneed cowardice but rather a positive determination not to perpetuate and foment enmity. Its efficacy as a practical policy has been proved beyond dispute in personal relationships on all levels.

The last point in this first section of the Sermon on the Mount makes an apparently impossible demand: "Love your enemies and pray for them that persecute you". Yet it has been done magnificently by many Christians from St. Stephen onwards (Acts 7. 54–60) and in modest ways by countless more. Love in the Christian sense has nothing to do with whether

166

we like people or not. We are not asked to like our enemies, or for that matter our neighbours. Still less has love anything to do with romanticism or lechery, sentimentalism or gush, as it is most commonly used in our own day. To love a person in the New Testament sense means to treat him as God treats us.

As Jesus says here there is no virtue in loving those who love us. Anybody could do that. But God makes no distinctions. Sunshine and rain are sent for the benefit of all alike, the good and the evil, the just and the unjust. So it is His will that all men and not only good men should be treated as His children, that we should be as ready to forgive as God Himself, and that we should be as concerned about the welfare of our enemies as of our friends. God's love to man is sheer goodwill. A Christian must try to see his enemies as well as his friends through God's eyes, and act towards them as God does. This is what Jesus means when He says that we must be 'perfect' as our heavenly Father is perfect.

Chapter Fifteen

A NEW KIND OF RELIGION

SO far Jesus has been dealing with our relations with one another. Now He turns to the question of our proper relationship to God (Matt. 6. 1–18). It is fundamentally a warning against any kind of self-advertising religiosity. If our gifts to charity, our churchgoing and our self-discipline are merely intended to win public approbation we may get that but we shall not get the approval of God. The practices that Jesus condemns are, of course, those current in His own day but the motives are timeless.

Charity is not charity if it springs from any other desire than to help someone in need. Jesus' well-known words at this point about not letting the left hand know what the right hand does are a picturesque way of saying that the best kind of giving for religious or charitable purposes is that which is known only to the giver. It would be foolish to suggest that Jesus thereby discourages any kind of charitable activity which has any element of publicity in it. This would indeed play havoc with countless worthy causes which publish subscription lists, with stewardship campaigns and the like. Jesus is not laying down rules but challenging us to consider our motives.

Similarly when He castigates as hypocrisy the practice of praying in public He is obviously not condemning public worship, in which He Himself took part in synagogue and Temple, but once again He is condemning a wrong attitude. Prayer is primarily a matter between a man and his Maker. The best kind of prayer is secret prayer and the best place to pray may at any given time be in a church, or in a room, or in the open air. When Jesus says we should always pray in a room by ourselves with the door shut, He means shutting the door of our minds to outward distractions and fixing our thoughts on God. We are not doing that if we are mainly concerned that our piety should be observed.

Next Jesus challenges ostentatious fasting. In the Jewish Church fasting was obligatory on prescribed occasions but extra merit in the eyes of the public could be gained by any who wished to acquire a reputation for holiness by letting themselves be seen with ashes on their heads and other signs that they were fulfilling this particular method of self-discipline. Once again Jesus is obviously not discouraging fasting or any other self-imposed act of renunciation but purely insisting that it should not be engaged in to win approval. In modern terms, to stop drinking or smoking in Lent can be good for the soul but the less said about it the better.

It is in this context of illustrating the wrong kind of piety that Jesus gives us in the Lord's Prayer the supreme example of how we ought to approach God. It is not by repetitive invocations nor even by the constant use of this particular prayer, but once more in the spirit rather than in the letter of the Lord's Prayer that we find our right relationship to God. In St. Luke's gospel Jesus teaches the disciples the Lord's Prayer in response to the request of one of them: Lord, teach us to pray (11. 1–4). The request was made by a man who had seen Jesus Himself at prayer and we may take it that in this pattern-prayer our Lord was passing on to His followers the lines along which His own prayers were offered.

The Lord's Prayer

In a sense the Lord's Prayer has as much to do with Jesus' teaching about God as with His teaching about prayer. Nothing is more revealing than the Aramaic word *Abba* which Jesus uses Himself in addressing God (Mark 14. 36) and which He here encourages His followers to use also. It is the affectionate everyday word for 'father' which a Jewish child would normally employ in talking to his parent. He would indeed

169

have been taught that God is his heavenly Father but he would never have used this word *Abba* for the Lord of Creation. Yet this is precisely what Jesus does and at once clothes the whole idea of God with new meaning. When we are told to say "Our Father", we indeed address One who is the Almighty, Sovereign Creator, but He is also One who loves and cares for all His children, who far more than any human father could do is ready to listen to us, understand us and forgive us.

This is the kind of God to whom we are to say: Hallowed be Thy Name. The Name of God in the biblical sense means the nature or character of God, so the point of the petition is the prayer that we may never fail to hold God in reverence, that we may never do or say anything ourselves which would bring the character of God into disrepute, and never condone anything which would encourage others to think of Him as less than the God Jesus has shown Him to be. God's Name is hallowed when the Church maintains the Faith delivered to the saints and when her members' lives reflect the spirit of Christ.

Then we are to pray: Thy Kingdom come. As we have seen, the idea of the Kingdom of God is central in Jesus' teaching. His invitation and challenge to men was to accept the sovereignty of God over their own lives, to become wholly obedient to Him as the life of Christ Himself perfectly exemplified. It must thus be the keynote of any Christian prayer that more and more, men and women everywhere should recognize that this is God's world and that the only true fulfilment of their lives is to commit themselves wholly to Him in complete trust and willing service. Clearly we cannot look for the full answer to this prayer in a world where the opposing forces of human pride and self-indulgence militate so strongly against the acceptance of the way of Christ, but the words express the conviction that in the end evil will be defeated and that God will reign supreme.

The next words are in effect part of the same petition: Thy will be done in earth, as it is in heaven. We can speak of the coming of God's Kingdom only if men are prepared to subordinate their own wills to the will of God. This is the chief lesson of Gethsemane. Jesus' will for Himself was not a Cross —how could it be?—but He accepted this bitter and untimely death as part of God's purpose for the world, a final act of obedience which the Son must carry through. When we can say: Our wills are ours to make them Thine, we have grasped the point of this part of the Lord's Prayer. To ask that God's will may be done on earth as it is in heaven, saves us from the fallacy of thinking that the Kingdom of God is some other-worldly reality, something that happens at the end of time. True, it is only beyond history and life as we know it that God's victory over evil will be finally assured, but we are plainly meant to pray and work for the spread of God's King-dom on earth by doing His will here and now. To pray this petition is wasted words unless we see it as primarily a personal call to service in the situation in which we stand.

Jesus teaches us to pray that God's Kingdom may begin to be realized on earth by people who are prepared to do His will, including ourselves. The vocation of the Christian is to co-operate with God to transform society on all levels— personal, social, economic and political. This is the divine commission. To our question, How can we possibly do this against such heavy odds? Jesus answers, in effect, By the power of God. God will supply your needs, forgive your fail-ures and give you strength. So in the next three petitions of the Lord's Prayer we are taught to ask for ourselves only what is necessary to enable us to do God's will.

"Give us this day"—not affluence, security, success, wisdom or saintliness but—"our daily bread"! Could anything be more down to earth? We have no claim on God, no right to expect even the privileges of the faithful retainer, nothing but what will keep body and soul together to enable us to do what we are charged to do. There is some difference of opinion as to whether the petition means: Give us our bread for today, or: Give us today our bread for tomorrow. Which-ever it is it makes little difference. Some have seen in the words a reference to the Bread of Life, Christ Himself, or a specific reference to the Eucharist. It is much more in keeping with the mind of Jesus to see in this petition a stark reminder that our requests for ourselves should be minimal.

The second thing we are to ask for ourselves is forgiveness. Again it makes little difference whether we say "forgive us our debts" or "forgive us our trespasses". Both mean what St. Luke's version of the Lord's Prayer more clearly describes as 'sins' (11. 4). This is a salutary corrective to the modern idea that sin is an old-fashioned and unpleasant word which is best forgotten. Why should we have a sense of sin? Clearly if we have no sense of sin we shall not ask for forgiveness. Yet Jesus says here unmistakably that we are all sinners. Whether we are conscious of that or not, the most complacent of us would be hard put to it to claim that we always do what we ought to do or that we never fail to live up to our best intentions.

The truth is that a sense of sin is the inescapable consequence of any honest examination of our daily actions and individual motives. The greatest saints have been most aware of failure. If we have avoided gaol, kept the Ten Commandments, "done no one any harm", we are still sinners who need God's forgiveness. How many things have we not done that we could have done, how much indifference have we shown to the crying needs of our fellow-men? Whether we think of sin as failing to pay our debt to those who love us, or the society that supports us, or as coming short of what we owe to God, Jesus makes it plain that we can expect forgiveness from God only in so far as we ourselves are ready to forgive others.

The third petition for ourselves and the last clause of the Lord's Prayer is: Lead us not into temptation, but deliver us from evil. This raises some problems. Would God be likely to lead us into temptation, and in any case is temptation not the inescapable accompaniment of living? Out of the many explanations and varying translations of these words the most likely meaning would seem to be: Help us not to be led into temptation. That is, we recognize that being the weak kind of creatures we are, capitulation is our most likely course unless we can draw on God's strength to resist.

Then we are told to add: Deliver us from evil. The words may mean "from the power of evil" or "from the power of the Evil One". Whether we think of evil as a personal or an impersonal reality we cannot deny that it *is* a reality, a force that is constantly pulling us away from God and the kind of life He would have us live. Again this is something that only the supernatural power of God which is stronger than evil can enable us to overcome. In His summing up of our basic needs: our daily bread, forgiveness for our failures and strength to fight the good fight, Jesus puts His finger unerringly on the fundamental truth about human nature, as in the first part of the Lord's Prayer He has pointed to the fundamental truth about God.

Christian Discipleship

So far, in Matthew's version of the Sermon on the Mount, Jesus has dealt with the proper relationship that should exist between a Christian and his fellow-men (5. 1–48), and between a Christian and God (6. 1–18). He now turns to the question of the proper relationship of the Christian to his environment (6. 19–34).

We are surrounded by a variety of things that are essential to any kind of life, Christian or non-Christian—money, food, drink, clothes, possessions in general. One difference, says Jesus, between Christians and non-Christians is to be found in their respective attitudes towards such things. A Christian can never make a god of any of them. They are all good in themselves and part of God's providential care for His children. There is no suggestion that we ought to be able to live without them.

What Jesus insists on is that material things should be kept in their place and that the moment they become our chief concern we have lost sight of the distinctive aim of the Christian

173

life which is to seek to know the will of God and to obey it. If a man has his priorities right and prosperity comes his way it will never stand between him and God. He will know how to use it. Jesus does not discourage foresight, planning for old age, or any other sensible safeguards against misfortune. He is reminding us of the limitations of any human planning. When He illustrates the point by drawing attention to the carefree life of the "fowls of the air" and the "lilies of the field" He is not commending a Micawber-like philosophy of life, but emphasizing the futility of making self-preservation an obsession. Death, ill-health, or financial ruin may overtake any of us at any time. If the whole purpose of our life has been a frenzied attempt to anchor ourselves securely to the world we live in we are living in a fool's paradise.

The last part of the Sermon on the Mount (7. 1–27) seems to consist of a variety of topics which Matthew has included at this point. All of them are of primary importance in any attempt to reach an understanding of the thought of Jesus. A Christian will not sit in judgment on his neighbour, for he will be only too conscious of his own failings. Since he himself looks for God's forgiveness he will try to see the faults of his fellow-men as God sees them. This of course has no reference to the execution of justice in which the judge acts on behalf of society, nor is it a ban on criticism of what we believe to be sub-Christian activities by our neighbours or by the community. It is primarily a demand that we exercise charity in our treatment of those who wrong us.

Jesus enunciates the Golden Rule as the sovereign guide to conduct and the essence of Old Testament teaching: "Always treat others as you would like them to treat you." We may take our cue from the generosity we receive ourselves at the hand of God, who gives freely and without stint. A Christian is known by his actions, not by his profession of faith. At the Day of Judgment we may claim that our religious activities entitle us to preferential treatment, but what will count then is the kind of life we have lived. Jesus concludes the Sermon

with a striking contrast between the man who heeds His words
and the man who disregards them. The first man builds his life
upon rock, the other upon sand. Our attitude to Jesus' words
is therefore our response to the supreme challenge of our lifetime.
The choice we make brings either salvation or damnation.

The Sermon on the Mount is far and away the most important summary of the teaching of Jesus but we can learn something also from the other four blocks of sayings which Matthew
has collected. In ch. 10 Jesus is concerned mainly with the
meaning of Christian discipleship. He sends out the Twelve
with authority to preach and heal. It is to be a short and swift
pilot scheme for the later missionary activities of the apostles,
hence Jesus' instructions are that they should travel light and
waste no time over the unresponsive.

He looks forward to the day when the mission of the Church
to the world will have begun in earnest and sees persecution
and martyrdom ahead. The disciples of Jesus cannot expect
any better treatment than their Master has received. House-
holds will be divided through the allegiance of one or another
member of the family to Christianity. In this sense Jesus brings
not peace but a sword. Yet the primary allegiance of the
true disciple is to Christ and not to his family. Elsewhere Jesus
speaks of those who do the will of God as His brother, sisters
and mother (Matt. 12. 50). The Christian life involves self-
sacrifice, but it is only through self-giving that we know what
life truly means. In this uphill and discouraging struggle to
win the world for Christ, His followers need never be dismayed.
The Spirit of God will teach them how to answer their accusers and the Father who takes note of every sparrow that
alights on the ground cares much more for His own children.
To offer a cup of cold water, the absolute minimum of charity,
to the most obscure follower of Christ is an action that will
not go unrewarded, and to acknowledge Christ as Lord here
and now brings acknowledgment by Him hereafter in the
presence of God.

The third 'discourse' of Jesus is a collection of parables

(ch. 13). All of them in one way or another have as their theme the Kingdom of God. It is not always easy as we read them to tell what may have been the actual words of Jesus and what is the contribution of the evangelist or earlier tradition. But the general import is clear enough. In the parable of the Sower, Jesus speaks of the differing responses to His message that God has now come into human life in a new way, challenging men to commit themselves to Him in love and service. There are those who say, We have heard all this before. There are the emotionalists whose allegiance is short-lived. There are those who understand Christ's message only too well and are not prepared to pay the price of discipleship. But there are also those who hear and respond in greater or lesser degree and who make up for all the rest. The experience of Jesus has been duplicated throughout the history of Christianity and His realistic appraisal of the human situation has saved many a discouraged and dispirited teacher and preacher from despair.

In the parable of the Wheat and the Tares, Jesus uses the analogy of the farmer whose enemy sows weeds among his crops to teach that we must never expect the Church to be a community of saints. Good and evil will exist side by side until the Day of Judgment. On the other hand the tiny beginnings of the Rule of God—the twelve disciples, one of whom was a traitor—would, like the little Mustard Seed, grow into vast proportions. The Good News would be like yeast in the baking of bread, permeating society until its effect would be felt everywhere.

Nothing in this world is so important as coming into the right relationship to God. Jesus describes this as comparable to the joy of the man who finds a Hidden Treasure or a Pearl of Great Price. It is worth all that we have to possess it. Even if, like a Drag-net which gathers in fish of varying quality, the Church consists of a mixture of good and bad, its strength will lie in having enough teachers who can see God's revelation as a whole, who proclaim the Acts of God from the Creation to the coming of Christ as one great divine purpose for the wellbeing and renewal of the world. They are like the Householder who brings from his store things new and old. Jesus insists, as we should say today, on the unity and uniqueness of the old and new Covenants or Testaments as the key to the understanding of the Kingdom of God.

Christian Charity

In ch. 18, the fourth block of the teaching of Jesus in Matthew, the dominant theme is Christian behaviour. It begins with the words which we have already noted (p. 157). Jesus has been asked by the disciples: Who is the greatest in the Kingdom? His reply is to bring a small child into the circle and declare that only a childlike trust and dependence upon God will qualify a man to enter the Kingdom. The greater his humility the higher will be his status in the sight of God. Jesus then utters a warning against leading weaker brethren astray and stresses again that to enter the Kingdom is worth any sacrifice. Then in one of these superb and unforgettable illustrations He likens God's care and concern for every sinner to the shepherd who leaves his other ninety-nine sheep to search for the single wanderer. Some words which follow reflect problems of discipline in the early Church rather than the actual teaching of Jesus but they lead into one of our Lord's greatest sayings: "Where two or three are gathered together in my name, there am I in the midst of them."

Two vivid utterances underline Jesus' demand that His followers should be as ready to forgive one another as God is ready to forgive us. Peter asks the Master how often a Christian should be expected to forgive someone who has wronged him and suggests seven times as a reasonable limit. Jesus will have none of this arithmetical calculation in human relationships and sets the limit at seventy times seven. In other words Christian forgiveness must have no limits. The parable of the Unforgiving Servant which follows tells of a man who had been absolved from payment of a large sum of money which he owed his master but who refused to overlook a trifling sum which was owed to himself. No mercy is shown by his master to this unmerciful character. Likewise, says Jesus, as in the Lord's Prayer, we cannot expect forgiveness at God's hands unless we have ourselves been ready to forgive others.

The fifth and final discourse of Jesus (chs. 24–25) has as its theme the Last Judgment. It is most unlikely that in its present form it reproduces verbatim what Jesus had to say on this subject. Schweitzer was right to insist that we cannot eliminate from the record of Jesus in the gospels anything that strikes us today as a jarring reminder that He came as a first century Jew and shared the beliefs of His times (see p. 14). But by the same token when we encounter here as in Mark 13 second-hand imagery which was the stock-in-trade of any Jewish apocalyptist from the book of Daniel onwards, we may be permitted to doubt whether in these chapters we have nothing but the original words of Jesus. More likely this last discourse consists of genuine utterances of Jesus about the Fall of Jerusalem, the Last Assize and His part in it, with sundry other relevant parables and sayings, plus the Jewish-Christian missionary element which one would expect, and can generally detect, in this particular gospel.

The general expectation of the early Church was that the new Age which Christ had inaugurated would be consummated by the end of the existing world and the Second Coming of Christ. Inevitably they thought of this event as liable to happen soon and the teaching of Jesus seemed to confirm it. God's victory over evil was as good as won. The final visible demonstration of this would brook no delay. Yet when the world did not come to a speedy end and Christ did not return, the faith of the Church was unshaken, which suggests that they looked again at the words of Jesus and saw in them a deeper significance than had at first appeared.

Jesus believed and taught that the fulfilment of His destiny as Son of Man lay beyond the suffering and death of Calvary. As Head of the new community which accepted the Rule of

God He would guide the life of the Church through His Holy Spirit, but when the gospel had been preached to all nations, in God's own time the present world order would come to an end. That end would involve the defeat of evil and the perfect realization of the Rule of God. To describe this, the only possible language was pictorial, poetic and symbolic, which inevitably opened the door to misinterpretation when it was treated as literal prediction and which invited emendations from well-meaning editors and evangelists.

It is with this in mind that we ought to see in the last great discourse of Jesus not a programmed sequence of events at the end of time and history but certain basic assertions about the meaning and purpose of history, the nature of the Christian life, and the ultimate Triumph of God. History moves onward to its climax which is the restoration of a fallen world and its total reconciliation to God. In this Christ sees Himself as the key figure. In parable and symbol Jesus stresses the need for Christians to be alive and alert to the great issues that confront them every day. The daily choices that we make to further or defeat the purpose of God have ultimate significance for our own lives and the life of the world.

Christ comes again to those who would be His followers in the day to day business of living just as He judges our daily failures to respond to His challenge. His Second Coming "in his glory and all the angels with him" and the Last Judgment are themes to be handled by poets and painters. Art can express basic truths which are ill-served by cold prose. Yet out of all this imagery the essence of the Christian life emerges superbly. We are recalled from the contemplation of the unimaginable splendour of Christ enthroned to the practical burden of His teaching—the care of the hungry, the lonely, the sick and the outcast. When we argue with characteristically evasive self-justification: Lord, when have we ever failed in our service?, Christ answers, "Inasmuch as ye did it not unto one of the least of these my brethren ye did it not unto me" (Matt. 25. 45).

Chapter Sixteen

THE MEANING FOR TODAY

WE must turn now finally to the crucial question, what do the life and teaching of Jesus mean for the twentieth century? It has been argued in this book that despite the fact that the record of Jesus' works and words in the New Testament has been transmitted in a form which makes it impossible to say with certainty, This is precisely what happened, or, That is undoubtedly what Jesus said, nevertheless the general picture of the kind of Person Jesus was and the kind of things He did and said emerges clearly enough to satisfy any reasonable inquirer.

It would be foolish, however, to pretend that this solves our problem which is basically more fundamental than the question of whether we can be satisfied that the gospels provide us with a Jesus of history. For when all is said and done, allowing for the fact that biblical language is often poetic, symbolical and mythological, and that any attempt to define or describe God is bound by the very limitations of the human mind to be inadequate, there does seem to be an irreconcilable difference between the biblical interpretation of the relationship between God, man and the ·universe and present-day reluctance to accept the idea of the supernatural at all.

Even if we rightly say that the question of whether God is 'up there' or 'out there' would not have troubled the biblical writers, who would have been equally convinced that He is 'down here', the fact remains that the God whom the Bible depicts, whether in the words of Jesus or of the Old Testament prophets, is a supernatural transcendent God, Creator, Sovereign and Lord of all life and history. It may be that if they had understood such definitions of God as The Ground of our Being or Ultimate Reality—if indeed these terms mean anything at all—they might have accepted them as a partial and inadequate attempt to express the truth about the rich and colourful living Person who was what the word 'God' meant for Abraham, Moses, David and Jesus.

By the same token the current description of Jesus as The Man for Others might have been accepted by the Apostles, by St. Paul, and by the other New Testament writers as part of the truth about Jesus. But surely such a definition does less than justice to what Jesus Himself said and did, and to the impact He made upon those who were closest to Him. It is one thing to say that self-giving is the keynote of the life of Jesus, but it was something more than that which made men call Him Son of God, the Second Adam, the Word Made Flesh.

The Bible is unashamedly anthropomorphic. God is a father, a husband, a shield or a rock—Christ sits at His right hand—underneath us are the everlasting arms. Yet there is never any suggestion that these are anything more than helpful human analogies which enable us to comprehend to some extent truths which are beyond our normal understanding. They are an attempt to convey in terms of this world things that belong to a different order of being. We do not sidestep this distinction by relegating the biblical conception of a three-tiered universe to the realm of mythology. The particular cosmogony which the biblical writers accepted does not affect their conviction that there are two orders of being, divine and human, that man is a creature subject to a Creator, who is not only present in what He has created but who stands above and apart from it.

This concept of an immanent and transcendent God is basically no more difficult to accept in the twentieth century than it always has been. Nor is there any more reason why we should dismiss the idea of a transcendent God because astronomy and space-travel have upset popular conceptions of God as being 'up there' or 'out there', than that Christian morality should be relegated to the junk-heap because modern man finds it uncomfortable. We have learned in the past century how to take the Bible seriously without taking it literally, but there are certain foundations of biblical thought which cannot be shaken without threatening to topple the whole edifice, and the belief in a personal transcendent God, a Person in heaven, however we conceive of it, would seem to be one of them.

The Bible claims that the gulf which exists between the Creator and His creatures has been bridged once and for all by the Incarnation, Life, Death and Resurrection of Jesus Christ, and the evidence of the gospels points us unmistakably forward to the historical confessions of the faith of the Church in one God, Father, Son and Holy Spirit. Even if we accept that the creeds of the Church are, like the Bible itself, an attempt to express the inexpressible, the life and teaching of Jesus can only be adequately accounted for as deriving from the life of the Trinity. Anything less than that reduces the teaching of Jesus to the level of words of an inspired Jewish rabbi which can have no particular claim on our attention, while His Birth, Resurrection and mighty works disappear into the realm of legend or mythology.

It was not this kind of diluted humanism that launched the Church and sustained it through its chequered past, and it was not this kind of emasculated gospel which has changed men's lives, inspired social reformers, saints and martyrs, stimulated poets, painters and musicians, and won the allegiance of learned and simple, old and young of every race and colour for almost two thousand years. It has rather been the conviction that in Christ we are confronted with the truth about ourselves, about God, and about the world in which we live. It has been the belief that Jesus is the Way, the Truth and the Life for all men at any stage in history: that men can stake their lives on such words as: "He that hath seen me hath seen the Father," or "God so loved the world that he gave his only begotten Son, that whosoever believeth in him should not perish, but have eternal life."

The power of Christ over the minds of men and His influence on the history of the world can only be explained within the framework of a full-blooded gospel which to many today seems old-fashioned. Yet it has stood the test of time. To say that we live on a visited planet, however we express it theologically, is basically true. "God came down to earth from heaven" is a statement which is obviously symbolic, like the statement that the sun 'rises' and 'sets', yet both statements are meaningful, and for ordinary purposes how better could we express them?

God was in Christ

Some words of Vincent Taylor in *The Person of Christ*[1] are relevant here: ". . . In becoming man, the Son of God willed to renounce the exercise of divine prerogatives and power, so that in the course of His earthly existence, He might live within the necessary limitations which belong to human finitude. Divine attributes of omniscience, omnipotence, and omnipresence were laid aside, not in the sense that they were abandoned or destroyed, but in such a manner that they became potential or latent because no longer in exercise. The knowledge of His heavenly origin and divine nature was given to Him by revelation and intuition, at His Baptism, Temptation, and Transfiguration, and during seasons of prayer and communion with His Heavenly Father. These experiences were remembered and formed the undertone of His life and ministry, but they were not always so central in His consciousness as to preclude the frustrations, disappointments and trials of a truly human life . . . Nevertheless, at all times, in His humiliation as well as in His exaltation, He receives through communion with His Father an impress upon His human consciousness which is the secret of His moral elevation and of His power to do 'mighty works' . . . "

This view would seem to be wholly in accordance with the evidence of the gospels. Whether we speak of "two natures in

[1] pp. 287 ff.

one Person" or "two sides of Jesus' personality" the impression made upon us by the record of the four evangelists is not one of "God dressed up as a man," but of a man whose deeds and words were in some extraordinary way invested with a power and an authority which were more than human. In this sense the miracles and the major personal experiences of Jesus find their explanation in that the latent or potential power of the Son of God was for the moment fully exercised.

The miracles of Jesus are thus not interruptions of the laws of nature but 'signs' of God's relationship to men—Lord of the winds and the waves, His purpose is nevertheless to heal broken bodies, restore deranged minds and turn death into life. This is what God does. The acts of Jesus in befriending the outcasts of society, in breaking down the barriers of race and class are windows into the purpose of God. His supreme sacrifice whereby He laid down His life for His friends is the clue to a God whose omnipotence is that of love, who suffers with those who are the victims of the world's evil. His Transfiguration and Resurrection are our ground for hope in life beyond the grave.

Much has been said of the "scandal of particularity" in respect of God's revelation of Himself in Christ. The time-conditioned setting of the gospel in first century Palestine, with carpenter's shop, fishermen and Pharisees as the stage props of an utterly antique Jewish scene, enacted in a pre-scientific age, has been felt by many to be an unsurmountable barrier to relating the words and deeds of Jesus to the modern world. But it is this very 'particularity' of the gospel, its localization in a specific segment of time and in the experience of a single generation of men and women belonging to a specific nation, that gives it a quality of timelessness, far more than if it had been handed down as a series of general principles and propositions embedded in an abstract setting.

The message of the gospel, springing from a concrete situation, carrying a conviction and an urgency that can arise only out of a living experience, has that same universal quality as the message of those poets and painters who have been most notably localized and time-conditioned. Raphael's Madonnas are no less the expression of a beauty that is eternal because he dresses them like Italian peasants, and Robert Burns is not less but more of a universal lyrical genius because his daisies are those of an Ayrshire field and his banks and braes are those of his own native Doon.

The life and teaching of Jesus confront us in the twentieth century in the same challenging way as they did the men and women of the first, tenth and fifteenth centuries, and as they will no doubt continue to do until the end of time. However much our world view may have changed since the days of the Roman Empire, it is still the same world and we have still the same human nature. We still have to come to terms with life, we are still subject to fear and anxiety, we still have to cope with injustice and suffering, and we still have to die. Human relationships in the family and the community present us with the same problems now as they have always done. Questions of who we are, why we are here, where we are going and how we may get there still demand an answer.

Christianity has never claimed to provide all these answers but it can claim to offer in the life and teaching of Jesus a signpost pointing to a way of life that millions of men and women have found meaningful, purposeful and exhilarating. To know that the universe is not in the hands of some impersonal force or at the mercy of chance but that it has been created and is sustained by One whom we can call Father, whose nature is love, whose concern is the wellbeing of all His creatures, is to have an anchor which enables us to ride out the storms which sometimes threaten to engulf us. Through Christ we know not only what God is like, we know also that in the life of the Church which He has founded, in worship, prayer and sacrament, the power of God is available to us for the day-to-day business of living and that it prepares us for the infinitely richer experience of life hereafter.

But what of this day-to-day business of living? Does the teaching of Jesus give us all the guidance we need? The answer is Yes and No. It is obvious that the teaching of Jesus is no clear-cut ethical system, no list of rules to be observed, no exhaustive *vade mecum* to the difficulties of life in a twentieth century world. If we are faced with the problem of a godless state, as were the German Protestants during the Hitler era, and look to the teaching of Jesus for explicit instructions on how to behave, we find the cryptic counsel to render to Caesar the things that are Caesar's and to God the things that are God's. It was thus possible for the so-called German Christians to support Hitler. On the other hand those who advocated a Confessional Church defied the government, and many of them ended in prison or were executed. The majority, however, let events take their course and sailed with the wind. All could claim that they were obeying the gospel teaching.

It must perplex or amuse non-Christians to note that within the same Christian congregation there may be pacifists and Territorial Army enthusiasts, teetotalers and *bons viveurs*, anti-gambling fanatics and men who have a standing account with a local bookmaker, Conservatives and Socialists who would argue that their particular party most closely conforms to Christian teaching, together with considerable divergence of views on divorce, and, more recently, on sexual relations outside marriage.

We may reply by saying that Christians who take the teaching of Jesus seriously must in the modern world unite in condemning war, since the concept of a just war in an age of H-bombs has ceased to have any meaning, and that they must regard drunkenness, gambling mania, anarchy or a police state, broken homes or sexual promiscuity as a travesty in any Christian community. But we must accept, and welcome the fact that there is an area of freedom in Christian behaviour in which, within the pattern of relationships to God and our neighbours which Jesus has established, there may be variation in the response which an individual makes, depending on his assessment of the situation. This, in turn, will depend on such factors as heredity, environment, sensitivity, physique and temperament.

Obviously no Christian can argue that the teaching of Jesus entitles us to follow our inclinations. Self-control and self-discipline are incumbent upon anyone who professes to be a follower of Christ. But as St. Paul, who understood the mind of Christ better than most of us, reminds us, Love is the fulfilment of the law (Rom. 13. 10). He points us back to the words of Jesus, in which He sums up the essence of Christian behaviour, singling out from the multiplicity of moral injunctions which He had inherited, the two commandments which seemed to Him to be paramount (Mark 12. 30–31): Thou shalt love the Lord thy God with all they heart, and with all thy soul, and with all thy mind, and with all thy strength (Deut. 6. 5), and, Thou shalt love thy neighbour as thyself (Lev. 19. 18).

This would suggest that to love God and our neighbour to the uttermost is the ultimate guidance that Jesus gives us, the compass by which we plot our direction, but that we are left to ourselves to decide how this operates in any given situation. In a sense this is true, and we have the well-known words of St. Augustine to confirm it: "Love and do what you will" or, probably more accurately: "Love and *then* do what you will". This, however, is by no means all the guidance Jesus gives us. If it were, being masters of self-deception as we all are, we could certainly claim the sanction of love to God and our neighbours for many a dubious deed.

What Jesus gives us in the Sermon on the Mount and elsewhere in His teaching is a picture of the kind of behaviour that we should produce if we were wholly obedient to God— humility, loving-kindness, compassion, purity of heart and mind, absolute honesty and integrity, and complete self-denial. But only one Man has ever achieved this, Jesus Himself. He beckons us to follow in His footsteps, and by the grace of

God, we may in our lifetime take a few faltering paces towards Him. But complete obedience to God is something that even the greatest Christian saints have never claimed to reach. It presupposes a Christ-likeness which may be achieved in the life to come but is beyond our range as mortal men.

But while Jesus sets us this impossible standard which we nevertheless must strive to attain, He assumes the validity of the Ten Commandments as a workable standard for normal day-to-day living. When the rich man asks Him how he can come into the right relationship to God, Jesus tells him to keep the commandments—not to commit murder or adultery, not to steal or slander, not to cheat or bring disgrace on his family. Only when the man claims that he has always observed these rules of life does Jesus put His finger on the particular weakness which has made him a frustrated and unhappy man, his love of money. When Jesus advises the man to get rid of his wealth it is because it is obviously that that is troubling his conscience (Mark 10. 17–22).

Similarly when Jesus in the Sermon on the Mount takes the commandments separately and shows that to keep them properly involves more than simply avoiding the acts of murder, adultery, perjury and so on, He is not encouraging us to murder so long as we do not hate, or to be promiscuous so long as we do not intend to be unfaithful, or to be free to break our word so long as we are generally trustworthy. He takes it for granted that we do not commit the overt acts, but shows that the right relationship to God and our neighbours demands even higher standards.

If we are to take the teaching of Jesus seriously, we must recognize that it is simply not true that we are left to judge each situation in the light of the overruling principle of love, and to act accordingly. Jesus' teaching is that in any circumstances certain things are always wrong and He gives a fairly comprehensive list of them—"evil thoughts, acts of fornication, of theft, murder, adultery, ruthless greed, and malice; fraud, indecency, envy, slander, arrogance and folly" (Mark 7. 21–22).

While love is the fulfilment of the law, and charity is the supreme virtue for the Christian, there is thus nevertheless a substantial amount of guidance given by Jesus to those who try to follow the Christian way of life. Coming back to our earlier examples, the gospel will not tell a man whether he should be a pacifist or a bomber pilot. It would be more likely to tell him to be a stretcher-bearer. It will not justify total abstinence, asceticism or Sabbatarianism, though it will suggest moderation in eating and drinking, and respect for our neighbour's right to a weekly day of rest. It will not tell us which way to vote but it will call on us to make a responsible decision to support the party that seems most likely to promote the general wellbeing of the whole community. It will say that divorce is not in accordance with the will of God, but it will not sentence a man and woman whose marriage has broken down to a lifetime of unhappiness. It will say that unchastity inside or outside of marriage is always wrong for those who are committed to be followers of Christ, but it will urge us to exercise the compassion of Christ in dealing with offenders and most of all with the problem of the 'fatherless' child.

If we were to single out from the teaching of Jesus any words which might seem to crystallize best the essence of what it means to be a Christian we should probably not do better than to take as our guide to life the two parables of the Good Samaritan and the Prodigal Son (Luke 10. 25–37; 15. 11–32). It has often been pointed out that the Good Samaritan had a simple problem: a wounded man needing help, and enough money in his pocket to see that the man was looked after. Modern life is much more complicated. It is not always clear what we should do and how we should do it, even if we are convinced that in the spirit of Christ's charity something ought to be done.

Yet the basic teaching of the parable is that if we accept Jesus' injunction that one of the two primary obligations for a Christian is to love his neighbour as he loves himself, and that means one hundred per cent, then the reply to the question:

Who is my neighbour? is simply: Anybody who needs help. The compassion of the Samaritan overrode his reluctance to help a hated Jew. His human sympathy for one of God's creatures reproached the scruples of the two ecclesiastics in the story who "passed by on the other side", no doubt for reasons that seemed to them at the time to be extremely sound. 'Compassion', 'charity', the 'cup of cold water', "inasmuch as ye did it unto one of the least of these my brethren ye did it unto me"—these are haunting and disturbing words. They pierce the armour of our self-defence and self-esteem and shake us into an awareness that it is our compassion and not our churchgoing, our charity and not our credal correctness, our helpfulness and not our ecumenical enthusiasm that shows whether we are Christ's followers.

The story of the Prodigal Son is the other half of the picture. The parable of the Good Samaritan illustrates our proper attitude to man, the parable of the Prodigal Son points to our proper attitude to God. However mindful we are of our obligations as Christians and however hard we try to fulfil them, the end of each day brings the recognition of how little we have succeeded. Our Lord's searching words puncture our complacency: "Even so ye also, when ye shall have done all the things that are commanded you, say: We are un-profitable servants; we have done that which it was our duty to do" (Luke 17. 10). It is at this point, when we come to ourselves like the Prodigal and confess our failure, that Jesus' story assures us of God's acceptance of us as we are. "And he arose and came to his father. But while he was yet afar off, his father saw him, and was moved with compassion, and ran, and fell on his neck, and kissed him." This is the kind of God with whom we have to deal and it is from our proper response to such love, the humility that involves daily confession and asks daily for forgiveness, that the right kind of Christian behaviour springs.